AF176663

FSC
www.fsc.org

MIX

Papier aus ver-
antwortungsvollen
Quellen
Paper from
responsible sources

FSC® C105338

The OTHER Computer History.

Amazing, amusing, and experienced Stories around the development of the IT from the beginning until the Internet.

Computer:

A **computer** is a machine that can be instructed to carry out sequences of arithmetic or logical operations automatically via computer programming.
(From Wikipedia)

1. John von Neumann
   Computer Pioneer (1903-1957)

2, Hans Bodmer
   IT-Specialist (1939-

This book is a new version of the same title, which was first published in March 2021. The major changes are both sides of the cover and corrections of the spelling, grammar, and typographical errors.

However, the content of the book stayed the same.

Please note that English is not the author's native language. He is fully aware that the applied writing style is very personal. And so are his handling of sentences, forms, and punctuation marks: Very liberal.

The book was triggered by a conversation between the author with his son. Thank you, Stephan, for your motivation
Thanks also to my co-worker Werner Knecht for his important additions.

The services from Google, Wikipedia, and PONS were much appreciated. The help from Grammarly and LanguageTool was pertinent.

Copyright:
Hans Bodmer
All rights reserved.
Set and cover design; Hans Bodmer

Foto page 3: Picture of Hans Bodmer (presentation film from 1965 for the CDC6600 at CERN
https://videos.cern.ch/record/43172)

Publisher: BoD · Books on Demand GmbH,
Überseering 33, 22297 Hamburg, bod@bod.de
Print: Libri Plureos GmbH,
Friedensallee 273, 22763 Hamburg
ISBN: 978-3-7562-3381-6

The Computer Evolution in Pictures.

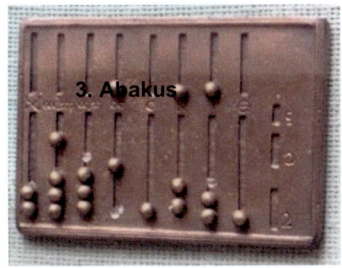

3. Abacus

4. Babbage Engine

5. Mechanical Bookkeeping Machine

6. Tabulator

7. Electronic Tube Calculator

8. Mainframe

9. Vector Computer

10. Super-Mini Computer

11. Personal Computer

12. Tablet

13. Smartphone

???

14. Future

Index

Prologue.

Question 1: What was the world before the Computers and THE NET?
There are not so many anymore who can remember that time. He can.
It was for a long time not realized what this 'thing' later called IT (Information Technology) did to the world. An entirely new dimension 'hit' humanity

Question 2: Could the impact of IT on the development of humans, the whole society, and almost everything, not be compared with the invention of gunpowder? Or even with the atomic bomb?

End of 'psychological' somersaults. Back to reality. Back to the text of 'The Other Computer History'.
What is coming now may not be of interest to many. Unless she or he is an extreme 'computer freak'. In 1955, there was no evidence of something like this. And also the ugly German word, 'Informationstechnolgie' was most likely not in the 'Duden'. 'Duden' was and still is the most important wordbook in German.
It was much easier, even for a born Swiss, to write the technical parts of what now is to be read in English. After all, English is the language of computer people. Not just for them. Children all over the world are eager to learn it already in kindergarten.
He is very, very familiar with the computer and everything related to it. Therefore, the 'DU' in the title of the German version of this book. The computer and he had been working together for 45 years. Sometimes friends, sometimes enemies. Deadly sad mood and joy followed in high frequent order. A kind of hate-love. It was definitely a very close relationship.
He was there. From the beginning. He was there until 2004 when he 'switched off'. Which means he wanted to forget everything about IT. With only half a success. As was so

often the case in his computer-oriented life. Today he is no longer so interested in the details of the almost crazy development of IT. And he's afraid of all its abuse.
He has become a normal user. But that too is becoming a burden. The daily battles with Microsoft Windows and Microsoft Word are getting harder every day.
But he's not (yet) completely out of service and away from that 'stuff'. In an intensive conversation with his son on his already somewhat advanced birthday, he recognized his defeats and victories with the machines which so frequently gave him big problems. But they also brought a lot of joy during his long professional career.

But writing it down is a very different 'story'.

It seems to have made a big impression on his son what he heard from his father. Of course, he is also a computer scientist. With a diploma and more. Not like his father. At his time, there were no signs of a possibility to study computer science. The term, as said, did not even exist. He has no official certificates. The only official document is the paper, which certifies that he has passed the exam in this hated profession as a precision mechanic.
 He received the certificate that he had completed his apprenticeship only after the second agonizing examination. And only because he made a sacred promise to the examiners that he would never work in this profession. Which he obviously would never have done.

In the 'Stone Age' of computers and data transmission, the universities did not see their future. The glamorous potential of the new techniques has long been ignored.
He saw it very early. But it was only by the conversation with his son that he realized what a great deal of knowledge he now has.

But does it bring something to write them down?

The question of all the questions: Does it bring money?
Is this not the only final criteria for almost every decision in

life?

This book will certainly not bring lots of cash!

He replied to his son: "No pig will care about my stories". The millions of young people who gesticulate today on laptops, smartphones, and whatever will come are only interested in the photo of the lover, dirty pictures, the games, the news about the next upcoming events and demonstrations,

"I am on Facebook, that's why I am". (Quote Rodolfo Bodmer).

So, it's a pretty hopeless project to write a book with forgotten facts about technical details. Or tell the world about the amazing moments he had together with a genius like Seymour Cray. Or the imagination you need to fix Supercomputers.
In addition, it will be extremely stressful to concentrate for two or more hours a day for weeks and months. Not to mention the dozen hours spent searching on the internet for forgotten abbreviations,
So, it's a pretty hopeless project to write a book with forgotten facts about technical details and their problems. Or tell the world about the amazing moments he had together with a genius like Seymour Cray. Or the imagination you need to repair supercomputers.
In addition, it will be extremely stressful to concentrate on correct names, verifying facts, and so on. And to fight the attempt to follow the guaranteed arising 'brain associations'. Force yourself to come back to the topic as soon as possible: To the Other computer history.
Yes, and let no mistakes creep in. A potential reader would not like this and the writer will receive malicious criticism. He prefers to leave mistakes to the computer. Or better to those who create the programs. The benefits of a computer are only as good as the programmer who wrote the software. A computer is a tool. Nothing else. Like a lathe. Only: To work with a lathe and to use it correctly has still to be done

manually.

Today, the computer is the boss. Nothing works without it. But also a lot goes wrong with it.

Quote: "The computer creates us today the problems which we earlier did not have".
Much about this unpleasant reality can be read from now on.
The beginning of the 'essay' was quite difficult. Will it ever be finished? Qui vivra verra!

Quote: "The spirit is willing, but the flesh is weak". (Matthew 26, 41 in the Bible).

Oh, excuse me for slandering the Homo sapiens. But like most things in life, the accused machine also has very excellent and useful skills. For example, It can perform calculations rapidly. Learning arithmetic in elementary school will soon become redundant. No more hated and strenuous learning of multiplication tables. The students need no longer construct grammatically correct sentences. They now have time to chat, send text messages and tell each other the usual nonsense. Or to play computer games. A very productive activity.
But without the word processor with all its 'features', problems, and errors, this text could never be written. Today, almost nothing is put on paper by human fingers.

In Switzerland, there is an important exception!
The last will !!!

1. It's hard to start…(1955-1961)

1.1. The beginning of his professional life.

He wanted to learn FEAM. It was in the late 50tis a highly
 desirable profession. Today, one would say top modern and
'in'. So, it is a job with a great future. FEAM stands for 'Fine
Mechanic and Electrical Apparatus Mechanic'. Well
understood: Mechanic and Electrical. Not electronic. A word
that just came up. The science behind this term was still a
long way from being accepted as such.
Let alone electronic data transmission. At that time, playing
with a remote-controlled toy car almost required a radio
license and learning how to signal in Morse. Is the Morse
code not the first one of the many more data transmission
protocols which will follow? It is some kind of 'semi-digital'.
The earlier smoke signals of the Indians, other old tribes,
and the medieval Swiss at the time of William Tell, were
analog
He had no chance to become a FEAM. As many times
before, he had no luck in his still short life. The
apprenticeship positions were very rare. And those who
were stronger than he had got hold of them. A little
brightness came. A company that trained FEAMs offered
him an apprenticeship as a precision mechanic. With the
option of being allowed to attend the theoretical schooling of
the FEAMs. This was nothing more than an empty promise.
Only to fill the unpopular apprenticeship position.
So, he struggled through this extremely unpopular ordeal.
Weeks of suffering from the filing of an iron block. The
exactness requested had to be within a hundredth of a
millimeter. The surface on the top of the iron cube had to be
exactly flat, as a special polishing machine, build to
accomplish this, could not do it better. And the iron block
was of extremely hard quality. When he was sweaty and
nerve-wracking, nearly finished, then the master punched
with a pointed iron hammer a huge notch into the now so

very fine edited surface. And the 'Sisyphean' work started again.

The only positive thing in the four-year apprenticeship was this: A colleague at work, two years older than him, remarked that he will never stay in the learned profession. He will go to one of the increasingly emerging companies that build electronic data processing machines. At that time, the term 'computer' was still very vaguely used. Better known were names like Burroughs, Honeywell, and a few more. And, of course, the largest and the leading one: IBM (International Business Machines). His colleague's statement remained deep within him. It was a sign from a higher power. In such a power, he does not believe it until today.

Is the idea to make a successful life with the 'things' named 'Computer' not only an illusion?

To quote Mark Twain: "Don't separate yourself from your illusions. When they are gone, you will continue to exist, but you will cease to live".

But it was definitely a tip that should have a major impact on his life

1.2. His first 'experiences' in the Swiss Air Force.

The reality then looked much darker. For example, he had to go through basic military training. He had to serve in the Swiss Army Air Force as a data transmission device mechanic. Their duties were, among others, to maintain the antique Siemens telex equipment constructed in 1939. Those worked with a data transmission rate of lousy 50 baud (bits per second). Baud is a term invented by Jean-Maurice-Émile Baudot.
The incoming messages were written on an 8 mm width and

10 meters long paper band. Or were punched with holes in narrow paper strips to be stored and to be able to resend the information. Those paper strips were later burned so that no military secret could get into the wrong hands.
The operating personnel, in the military term the BP2 (operating personnel 2) cut the printed paper strip together and glued them onto a normal sheet of paper. This page was then handed in strict confidence to the officer on duty. The UEMGTMs (Swiss military abbreviation for data transmission device mechanics) then wrote for fun love letters to their girlfriends on these paper strips just mentioned. They rolled them in tiny rolls, and then they were sent by the military postal service to the at that time favorite 'female'.

Then he had to deal with loud rattling mechanical encrypting devices. In bulletproof heavy iron boxes. And, as a telephone soldier, had to hang with a long hook kilometers of wires on roofs, trees, and lamp posts. Then he had also to establish telephone connections by plugging cables in the 150 kg heavy semi-mobile telephone switchboard. From time to time, the commander was, for great fun, connected to the nearest madhouse.
And, of course, also had to struggle through the usual soldier disciplines such as guard duty, goose-stepping, bodybuilding exercises, throwing hand grenades, cleaning the toilette, peeling potatoes, and so on. And was forced to march in nailed shoes, in the jargon called 'gearwheel sandals', on hard roads and through rocky trails. He still was equipped with the wooden carbine model 48. A very precise shooting riffle. If you could operate it correctly. He was very terrible at it. He felt the huge recoil after every shot. This resulted in a swollen shoulder and a sore collarbone.
This basic training, called the RS (Rekruten-Schule), was an agony. A lived nightmare. The 'experience' troubled him so much that it was causing bad dreams until old age.

1.3. Stockholm, Sweden.

But, like everything, the RS ended. He was again back in reality. Because of his lousy final apprenticeship exam, finding a job in Switzerland was out of the question. He definitely wanted to go abroad. But where? Sweden was one of the few options. At that time, roughly on the same wage level as Switzerland. So, he asked the Swedish embassy in Bern about the opportunity to work in Sweden. And promptly received a work permit as a so-called 'Staginare' and also a job offer from the LM Ericsson Company in Stockholm. This company built all sorts of electrical devices, telephones, etc. And of course, the most lucrative: The weapon systems.

The first month in Sweden was very hard. Not so much the work. This was more or less feasible. But the climate! Especially a winter with 1.5 hours of sunshine throughout the entire month of January. This fact was proven by the meteorological office of the city! The food, respectively for him, rather a diet for the very poor's, was also anything else but a pleasure. Deep depression was announced and also came true.

His main job was to clean chassis for secret instruments in military airplanes. These frames were made of magnesium so that they, in an airplane crash, immediately burn, and no secrets could be detected by the enemies. It was boring, annoying piecework. Not too much stress: The excellently organized Swedish trade union was excellent at negotiating working conditions. But to profit from their support, he had to join the union and pay the contribution even with his small wage. This was the smallest possible by Swedish law.
But then there was a ray of hope. Not so much the highly anticipated spring. But in the form of a new job. The company Burroughs AB in downtown Stockholm was looking for service technicians for their mechanical calculators. 'Technician' is by far an exaggeration. It was

pure fine manual adjustment and assembly work. On fairly complicated mechanical desktop calculators. They were very slow and expensive. With dozens of tiny springs, cogwheels, bent wires, finely turned pens, and so on. The thing was called 'Ten-Keys'. Because it had ten buttons to type in the operands. All the machine was able to do was add numbers. But this rather primitive machine (not a computer...) was sold well. In the absence of something better on the market.

At least, working with these machines was never boring. And often a real challenge. He loved those. But sometimes it was too much for him. His favorite saying was then: "Can that not be accomplished easier?" (In Swedish: Kan ni inte göra det lättarere?).

The month of August in Sweden was approaching. He didn't want to go through a second torture winter in Sweden. And he was sick and tired of the food there: Sandwiches (smörgos), blood sausage with raisins, red sugared sausages (grillard korv), not good tasting Christmas fish, weak beer (fatöl), and the strong potato schnapps. This only could be bought in a shop owned by the state, namely The 'Statlic Bolaget'. Especially before the festivity days, only after a long wait in the cold in a huge waiting queue outside the store.

•

1.4. His first Job as a Programmer.

So, it was time to go back to Zurich. Without money. Because there was another illusion running down the drain. Somebody told him that he would get returned the contributions he paid for the old-age pension plan in Sweden when he leaves the country. But this was not so. Only much later were 127 crowns and 50 öre (About 100 Swiss francs) transferred to Switzerland.

So, he is returning to Zurich by hitchhiking and living on bread and water. Then he had to find a job. With, to say the least, not the best certificates.

But for once, he was lucky. At least apparently. The company Burroughs, again the same one as he worked for in Sweden, was looking for programmers for their accounting machines. It was so stated in the job advertisement in the newspaper.

And he was hired!

It will surely be very fascinating to 'make' programs for these mechanical 'monsters'. With a weight of over ten kilos. They look like a giant typewriter with over a hundred keys. The programs were not written but were 'cut'. The commands to achieve the desired processes were controlled by the 'presence' or the 'absence' of a 5x5 millimeter in size small iron plates. Depending on the command of the program to be executed, those were snapped off at the lower edge of a 20x50 millimeter plate with a pair of pliers. These plates were then placed in a 50-centimeter-long frame underneath the sliding 'wagon' at the top of the machine. This 'wagon' slides relative quickly from right to left of the machine. Underneath this moving part, are small mechanic sensors scanning the prepared little plates. These sensors in turn trigger the functions of the other mechanical elements in the machine. They will finally execute the desired calculations.

Unfortunately, the reality looked much more unpleasant and darker. He was not allowed to 'enjoy' more than 5 percent of his working time in designing and 'cutting' programs. The remaining 95 percent he 'suffered' as a representative (or better: As door-to-door salesman) for mechanical calculators. The same 'Ten-Keys' he earlier repaired in Sweden. In the hot summer, wearing an uncomfortable perspiration caused polyester suit, white long-sleeved shirt, and red tie. He had to knock on the doors of the very expensive offices in the main business street in Zurich, namely the Bahnhofstrasse. To get thrown out again and again by the secretaries. Until one of the ladies shouted at him: "Young man, you better go to work!"

That was enough. He didn't sell anything. His superior showed something like pitying him. This is very usual in this kind of business. He sent him to a customer in a distant, remote village where a second-hand older 'apparatus' could be used. He was then able to sell such a 'crutch'. The only thing he ever sold in his life. It cost 100 Swiss francs. He is until today still ashamed to have made this deal. And he still suffers from a guilty conscience until today.

15. Punched Paper Strips

16. Paper-Tape Telex

17. Encryption Device

18. Swiss Air Force Batch

19. Ten-Keys Calculator

20. Mechanical Accounting Machine

2. At the 'Zenith' of the punched card 'Époque' (1962-1963)

2.1. The Compagnie des Machines BULL.

This promised job as a programmer at Burroughs turned, in fact, out to be, as said, a door-to-door salesmen job for outdated mechanical calculators. It was absolutely nothing for him. He had to find another employer as soon as possible. Something that at least satisfies and motivates. And which should also be reasonably well paid.

It wasn't easy. Despite that, the general economic situation was not that bad at that time. And there were also newspapers with dozens of job offers. One of those immediately caught his attention. A not so well-known French company, headquartered in Paris, the 'Compagnie des Machines BULL', was looking for service technicians for their products. These were mainly machines to process punched cards. In direct competition with the notorious leader in the upcoming IT business: IBM. And BULL was in many respects superior to the 'monster'. As was so often the case with products invented in France: Mongolfière, Caravelle, Concorde, Citroën DS19 and 2CV, Michelin tires, TGV, and others.

He called the company and was promptly asked to send the usual papers needed for a job application. And the grades achieved in the primary and secondary public school, the with a lot of luck obtained certificate as a precision mechanic and the references of his hitherto very poor and extremely unsuccessful professional career. Does he have more success this time? At least, he was invited for an interview and an aptitude test.

The Swiss subsidiary headquarters of BULL was near the Zurich main station. In a dry office building on the sixth floor. The aptitude test took place in a tightly furnished classroom. At the front table were the future bosses and others. They all were severely looking at the incoming candidates. It turned out that some of the examiners were experts in testing them for the job psychological suitability of the candidates. They were engaged as consultants to find out if the applicants had them for this position required practical and intellectual skills.

The candidates for the attractive job were seated behind small tables. All, as it should be, dressed in a suit and wearing a tie. This in the middle of a hot summer. Cleaned, washed, and combed like choirboys. And they were behaving like those.

In a strict command tone, it was announced that exactly one hour and not a minute longer will be given to solve the questions. The hour was started with a strong strike with a hammer at a gong bell. He started immediately. It was the first time that he had to undergo such a rigorous and important psychological test.

It was dead quiet in the room. Disturbed only by the experts who sneaked with a critical look at the candidates through the rows. Sure, It had to be checked that nothing was written off or otherwise cheated.

The tasks were, surprisingly, 'relatively' easy. The finding of logical explications in a series of numbers and symbols (pattern recognition) was demanded violently and overemphasized. Then simple arithmetic followed by questions about electrical terms like ohms, volts, amperes, watts, hertz, etc. Then they had to draw simple electrical diagrams and outline electrical circuits and the like. After this, colored numbers on a muddled paper had to be recognized. This is because it was needed to correctly differentiate the colored wires in punched card devices. And then the usual everyday questions followed by general historical, social, and political ones. This was to test the overall knowledge.

There was silence like in a cemetery in the room. Concentrated thinking was the order of the day. After about 50 minutes, he had completed the tasks. He looked toward the experts and signaled that he had finished the test. Astonished reaction from them. He was quoted with a sign of the hand to the man who was probably the highest boss in this forum. Then he was asked in a very strict tone:

"Did you recheck your answers thoroughly?"

He had.
"Are you sure about this?"
He was!

The man now whispered, politely and almost a little appreciatively: "You will soon be contacted by the chief of personnel of the Compagnie des Machines BULL, Switzerland".

The notification came very quickly. At last, something very positive. An invitation for a personal interview. This took soon place. It went very well for him. They offered him a job as a service technician. Condition: To be ready to attend a six-month training in Paris.

This was more than just great! He loved traveling and to see foreign countries. The wage was actually for him at that time of secondary importance. It was not at all disappointing CHF 1400.- per month. He had never earned so much before. Of course, there will be a three-month trial period. And if the grades achieved in the weekly tests are insufficient, then an immediate dismissal will take place.

They provided him with the coordinates of the

training center in eastern Paris. At the Avenue Gambetta to be precise. A list of nearby cheap hotels was also given. BULL can on request arrange the booking. The train ticket Zurich-Paris, of course, second class, was also sent to him.

The whole training phase in Paris, as previously stated, will last 6 months. Every month there is a two-day 'vacation' to take a break at home. Exams are held on Saturdays. The results are sent immediately to Zurich. Therefore, it was always possible to be fired. In the jargon, they say: 'Kicked out'.

2.2. The first 24 hours in Paris.

He could hardly wait to start the adventure. The train from Geneva to Paris took almost eight hours. It was much earlier than when years later the legendary TGV hisses to Paris in three hours. It was a gray January evening. Arrival at an equally gray and desolate train station, the 'Gare de l'Est'.
The hotel was located near the 'Butte Chaumont'. The escalator from the metro up to the street is very long and steep. The one-star, or better half-star, rated hotel was rather shabby. There was no dining room to be seen. Just a small bistro right next to the entrance. The lady at the reception desk was quite grumpy. Understandably, she had to work on a Sunday. Checking in was easy, then she had already all the information about the new guest. She gave immediately the following instructions: "No smoking in the room. Visits from women are not permitted. The house rules and the way to the emergency exit are posted in the room". Of course, in French. A language he was only very rudimentary familiar with. Three lousy years of secondary public school. The room was on the third floor. No elevator, but with a gnarled wooden staircase. The 'chambre'

was tiny. And so, the bed. The lighting was dim. Through the unclean window, he could see a small treeless park. Next to it was a kind of dilapidated garden. Surrounded by windowless, mismanaged buildings and decayed gray brick walls.

But what the hell: Does it matter?

He's only here to sleep. To do the sure upcoming homework, the small round red dusty table lamp equipped with a 40-watt light bulb will be enough. But first, unpack the suitcase, prepare them for tomorrow's necessary papers and the surely be needed special literature and the writing utensils. Tomorrow it will be his personal D-Day. But despite the fact that time had already progressed, and it was already getting dark outside, he still wanted to go out. To look for the future place of the schooling. So that he doesn't go astray the next morning and appear too late at the training center already on the first day. Fortunately, Avenue Gambetta was nearby and within walking distance. Will avoid the arduous 'metro stress' in the mornings.
The school building was very impressive. Tall and with shutters closed window. The house was surrounded by a high iron fence with only one very intimidating iron door. The whole complex looked like a prison. There was nothing written on the whole building. No sign or indication of what the building was for. Fear of rioters, terrorists, sabotage, or their like? This thought was causing a cold shower over his neck.

Back to the hotel. He needed badly a glass of beer. A 'Demi' as it was called there. In the still empty bar. After a long wait, a lady showed up. The same 'witch' as before at the reception. She pushed a jug of beer at him and wanted immediately cash.

The sleep that night was very much on the troubled

side. The waking up too. Quickly wet the face with cold water. Then get dressed. He had to bind the tie correctly. He polished his black shoes a little with the tablecloth. He went down for breakfast in the now awful, brightly illuminated room next to the bistro. The menu consisted of 'Croissants' without butter and lukewarm milk coffee in a large cup. What else could be expected here?

He was at the training center almost half an hour too early. A doorman in uniform looked skeptical (or is it spelled 'sceptical' ?) at him.
Then he checked the presented papers and examined critically his passport. Then he said: "You have to wait in the entrance hall until the responsible instructor will arrive".
Three young men about his age arrived. Also dressed very correctly. They spoke Swiss German among themselves. With an unmistakably Bernese accent. They are certainly his future classmates. Then came in two blond, tall guys. They chatted in Swedish. He noticed them all, but did not say a word. Now many more trainees appeared. But they are not new because they immediately went up the stairs to their classrooms.

At exactly 08h00, the entrance gate was closed by the doorman and locked with a big iron key. Those who come too late have no chance of getting in and will anyway be fired immediately.
The six new ones had to wait. The teacher let them suffer. But finally, he came. He greeted them in broken German. The group went up the stairs and into a classroom. Small but not bad. Big enough for the 6 men's team. They sat down. He, as it is usual for him, in the back of the room and alone in a row. First, the teacher introduced himself. Then an imposing appearance appeared. Probably the director of the whole training center. The man held his hands on the back. He greeted the new ones in

27

French. Very quickly and very emphatic. The subordinated 'teacher' tried to translate it into German. Not so quickly and not so correctly. The director explained the rules of behavior: Punctuality, secure appearance, discipline, accuracy, courtesy, friendliness, and so on. Reminded him of the speech by the commanding officer on his first day in the military basic training.

The director of the training center left the room with strict steps. The door closed firmly and with a lot of noise behind him.

He found that the translation by the class teacher was rather poor. Even with his meager French, he could have done it better. And then the instructor said this: "Das BULL service technician always wears a dark suit with a red tie and white shirt. Beards, snouts, and uncombed hair are not tolerated. And when das BULL technician buys a car, then he buys a black car". He always said: DAS BULL Techniker. Somehow he had a problem with the German grammar (Correct is: Der BULL Techniker). But the 'message' was clear: Prestige is most important!

The teacher now explained the schedule. First, there are two hours of theory. Then a short coffee break, followed by two hours of practical work on the devices. Then lunch breaks in the canteen, oh sorry, staff restaurant! In the afternoon, the same program again. Only without a subsequent meal. And then the teacher got down to what he was there for, namely to instruct the future maintenance technician.

2.3. The Card-Puncher and what can happen to it.

The first machine they will get to know, and he will later have to master, is the card-puncher. This device is a medium-sized machine covered with dark-gray painted sheet metal. Such machines were present in the classroom. Ready to be taken apart. The card-puncher works like this: On the top is a box in which the virgin cards are placed before they are fed in and punched. The holes are rectangular, measuring approximately 1.5 by 6 mm. The instructor explained that there is a punched card system that uses round holes. So applied by the competitor Remington Rand. This later became Sperry Rand and then Unisys

Only as a remark: Computer companies change names, swallow others, and then are swallowed themselves.

These punched cards with rectangular holes were developed by IBM. They were mechanically easier to read than the round ones. This is done by passing them under tiny brushes made of thin wires. The manufacturing of those requires the highest precision. Because an error when entering the data for processing would cause very catastrophic results in the further processes. After the numbers and/or characters have been entered at the keyboard by a data typist, mostly a female, then the needed holes are punched with steel stamps of again the highest precision. These expensive components get used up after a certain time and must therefore be periodically replaced. So that the holes do not 'fray out'!
The force needed to stamp the holes comes from a strong electromagnetic coil. A process that needs a

lot of energy. That is why the network part of a card-puncher is very voluminous. Another critical point is the positioning of the card in front of the stamps. Of course, this also happens mechanically. The problem is that only one card should be pushed in at a time. This again requires precise knife-like sliders and a very exact slit through which the cards were pushed. The device is producing quite a lot of noise.

He soon heard this. After the first weeks of studying the circuits, learning to measure the required electrical values, practical exercises to accomplish the proper adjustments, the 'apprentices' were immediately exposed to the real punched card-producing world. So to speak: Thrown into the cold water.
The place of action for him was a very well-known, famous bank in the Cité. Fortunately, he was accompanied by an experienced local technician. In a large, stately big hall with a high ceiling were about twenty card-punches lined up in rows. Behind the devices sat young women and older girls in black dresses which looked like uniforms. They were at first still inactive. They had their arms self-protectively crossed over their breasts. They chatted discreetly and quietly. At the desk in the front of the 'girls' stood a 'biblical' natural disaster. The long 'drought'. She must be the supervisor. She looked like he imagines a female guard in a detention center looks. The hair was tightly and strictly knotted at the top of her head. She had thick horn-rimmed glasses. Dressed in black long legs pants with perfect folds. And this in 1962! The authoritarian, fierce mine fitted her exactly.

At exactly 08h00, the 'show' began. The 'long drought' stretched her right hand up and shouted in a Prussian command tone. But of course in French: "Allez!!!"

30

Now the rattling started. The noise level in the hall achieved soon a higher level of decibels than normally would be allowed at a workplace. The ugly lady snaked very often back and forth between the rows. She made a warning remark here and there to one of the female 'slaves'. Or held up her index finger when she saw something she didn't like. And also probably to urge them to work faster and to be more precise.

After an hour, she shouted very loud the command: "Stop!"

The room became immediately dead silent. The commanding 'lady' stood up and demonstrated a grotesque exercise. This was to loosen the fingers and wrists. All the 'girls' stood up and tried more or less precisely to do the same. After five minutes, the 'theater' was over and the noise resumed. Now even louder than before.

His experienced companion and he were placed in a small room next to the hall. The door to it remained open. They were there to be immediately ready to intervene when one of the machines fails. Not one minute should be lost in this hectic 'factory'! Time is money. Which the bank had abundantly. While they were waiting for troubles, he read over and over again the instructions for the maintenance and the repair of the rickety machines.

And there were defects! More than he liked. It happened very soon. A little young lady at the back stood up. This was strictly prohibited. Not even to go to the restroom. She was chubby, unusually lively, with frizzy hair and with friendly blinking blue eyes. She gave the technicians a lively signal with the thumb pointing down. to indicate that her machine had a breakdown.

Her card-puncher stood still. Neither wobble nor noise. His tutor sent him to her. His first useful 'work' in his 'career' as a maintenance engineer.

31

The problem was relatively simple. A fuse had blown up. But now he had to try to find out the reason for it. This was done according to the regulations by carefully controlling all the components which could cause this fuse to blow. The checklist specifies more than twenty items that have to be examined in detail.

Despite the exact obeying of the regulations, there was no reason found for the 'accident'. So, there was also no reason for further actions. The whole 'exercise' took almost half an hour. During this time, the little card-punching-maid was sitting comfortably well on one of the chairs in the back of the room. With her arms crossed. She was apparently not very unhappy about the little rest that she received unintentionally. Looking at her, not entirely accidentally, he believed to have seen a certain mischievous smile on her lips.

But soon he was no anymore in the mood to smile. Because the unpleasant 'miss-happening' repeated itself after a little over an hour. His superior now looked at him impatiently and reproachfully. A shower of swear words followed. And then he was in public and in broken German offended. The boss, outraged, took now himself over the 'case'. To him, the beginner's relief and full satisfaction, the proven specialist also found no explicable reason why the same fuse always gave up.

After a short lunch break, the 'ritual' of card punching continued. He no longer sat in the adjoining room but at the back of the hall very near the wall. Apparently, flicking through a thick booklet. But he observed, without anyone noticing it, with very sharp eyes the young woman whose device was having these unexplained breakdowns. And which only occurred with her machine! And what he was waiting for happened. The whole agonizing scene arrived again very soon. By now, an objective explanation of what was the problem is urgently needed.

He had one!

He had it guessed. He saw that the little lady bent herself shortly over towards the floor to pick up a fallen-down datasheet. It was later found out that she deliberately dropped it! Now she opened very quickly the door which closes the chassis where the relays were located. She fumbled inside the machine for half a second. Then she hurried quickly back to the normal sitting position. And, wow, the machine was immediately coming to a standstill. She looked at him innocently like an angel. As if she were begging for help. He rushed toward her with sure steps. Politely, as instructed, he wanted to shake her hand and introduce himself.

Wanted to shake her hand!

She pulled hers jerkily, violently backward. Behind her delicate back. But what did he nevertheless see vaguely in her hand? A tiny metallic hair clip! Small enough to be clamped between the contacts of one of the large relays situated in the cabinet whose door she just had closed. She noticed that he has seen this. She nearly fell into a faint. Became pale like chalk. And then wrinkled red like a withering little bouquet of roses.
What should he do now? To accuse or even blacken somebody is not his habit. And the explanation of the breakdowns she deliberately provoked has now been found. He raised his index finger of his right hand violently and menacingly. The left hand he pushed over his mouth. To indicate that he will not say to others what he saw. She would have earned a very strict rebuke. But he only gave her an accusing look.
From there on, there was no need to replace fuses during the whole rest of the week. On the last day at

the bank, he was visibly relieved and was leaving the place even with a small little bit of pride. In the hallway, he felt a touch from behind on his right shoulder. His thoughts were already far away from the previously happened amazing story. They were at the coming week and the further new devices he will have to repair one day. Therefore, his turning around of this head to see the cause of the slap came with a delay.

Nobody could at first be seen. But now something very unexpected arrived. A nice small little packet was passed to him from the left. Must be from a woman's hand. From the hand of the pretty fairy dressed in a fashionable very nice summer skirt and who disappeared in a flash. Completely stunned, he immediately opened the gift with trembling fingers. A small envelope contained a card with a red rose. In it was, with golden letters, written: MERCI!

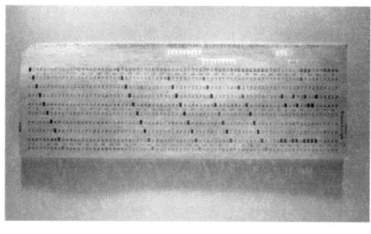

21. Punched Card

22. Card Puncher

2.4. The 'Vérificateuse', the 'Traductrice' and the 'Trieuse'.

The week in the Cité was over. The last 'episode' was the only positive of what happened. He will always remember this 'adventure' and the little 'rogue' forever.

Back to the training program. The next machine is very similar to a card-puncher, the in French called, 'Vérificateuse'. This is a machine to verify the correctness of the data on the previously punched cards. Control is essential! Because incorrect input data will surely severely spoil the results of the operations.

Quote from an unknown author: "Garbage in, garbage out"
Everybody involved in IT will thoroughly agree.

This 'rule of thumb' of course also applies to Supercomputers, Minicomputers, PCs, Laptops, Smartphones, and whatever will follow

On this verifying device, the previously punched cards are certified. The operator, again mostly female typists, now 'promoted' to 'controller', types again in the same values read from the original data list. If they don't match, then the person who produced the mismatch has a huge problem. Could result in a reduction of the surely not exaggerated salary. Or, in the worst case, end up in immediate dismissal. Hopefully, it will never hit the pretty little lady with the nasty hair clip.
This verifying machine is technically less demanding and much quieter than the card-puncher. The most important challenge is the positioning of the card to be read in. This has to be

done with high precision to avoid that the small metal brushes that 'read' the holes do not go through the wrong one.

Numbers or characters were with BULL's card-puncher were not printed on the card. This was done by the next device that he had to learn: The, in French, 'Traducteuse'. This machine is big as a kitchen chair without a backrest. And, like most of the punched card machines from BULL, very solidly built. And covered with gray painted sheet metal. The cards are again pushed in by 'knives' and scanned by the little brooms. Then they are moved further to receive the printing. This is accomplished with eighty 5 centimeters round and 3 millimeter wide discs which have the numbers and letters engraved on the outer edge. They are aligned on an axis and rotate with a high number of revolutions per second over a black typewriter ribbon. When the to-be-printed character is above the ribbon, then an electrically activated coil underneath is activated. It presses a 'hammer' against the card which is now positioned under the ribbon and the character is consequently printed.
The machine makes, when running, a very unpleasant noise, and the 'apparatus' is getting into jerky movements. This causes the whole machine to 'jump' up five millimeters.

This 'environmentally unfriendly' behavior didn't really bother him. More tedious was this: To control the printing process, he had to bend himself closely over the rapidly turning discs. And this dressed in a white shirt and the mandatory tie. The tie must be anchored behind the neck. Because the danger that the tie gets stuck in the fast rotating parts is huge. And could strangle you! The white shirt that has to be worn is also not ideal. The sleeves were for this work, of course, rolled all the way back. Very soon it will no longer be white, then drops of black ink are frequently sprayed all over the technicians. They were 'punished' while simply doing their job.

Next what he got to know was the in French, called 'Trieuse'. This is a machine to sort the punched cards. For example, sorted according to ascending order numbers, amounts of cash, credits, debits, or other such values. This device is now more modern than what he so far had 'experienced' or better 'survived'. It is about two meters long, thirty centimeters wide, and high enough to be comfortably operated. It is even partly made of the more expensive aluminum. The punched cards to be sorted are placed in a container at the right end side. They are then pushed at relatively racy speed by again fine 'knives' and then slide horizontally towards the other end of the device. There are twelve 10 centimeters wide compartments under the horizontal plate. Depending on the value punched on the cards, a 'slot' is opened at the right moment and the card drops into the intended compartment. After all the inserted cards are processed, then they are removed from the boxes by the operator. The operator takes the cards out of those and 'shuffles' them together by hand. Then the cards are fed-in again to be sorted by the next character. This process is executed so many times as the values had digits.

The 'sorter' is, compared with the devices he learned so far, technically not very challenging. Except for the adjustment of the knives and the very exact gap width of the slot for reading the cards is rather boring. It doesn't have to be that way. A little bit of fun must be.

But is not allowed!

But very simply achieved: Remove the electrical fuse for the magnetic coils which actuate the opening of the receiving boxes. So, all cards shoot to the end of the device. There you remove the end panel of the machine. That is effortlessly done by just unhooking it from two hooks.

And the inferno is unleashed

When the machine is now started, the cards 'fly' over the edge of the machine into the room. At the speed of over 20 cards per second. The floor will be littered with the tediously punched and verified cards in no time. Please, ladies, don't walk around it in high heels!
This for the 'trainees' very amusing 'effect' was not at all appreciated by the instructor: "Whoever produces something like this again will immediately be fired. Adieu!".

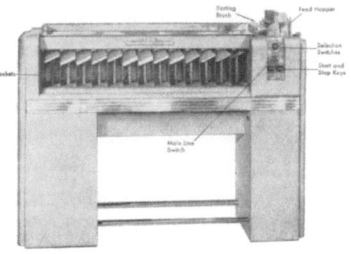

23. Trieuse

2.5. The mysterious Card-Mixer and the Tabulator.

The next device that the 'students' were facing is really a kidding one. A 'thing' that mixes the punched cards and punches holes in new ones. An extremely chunky structure. Very heavy and big. Again with iron frames almost as solid as railway tracks. This machine is somehow almost hopelessly mystical. There are compartments on both sides for feeding in the punched cards. There they are read in depending on the program and then intermixed. For example, three from the right compartment then one from the left, or vice versa, and/or in different quantities. In the middle is a container with 'virgin' cards, which then will be punched according to what the controlling program requests. This program, punched also on a card, is read in first. The commands that control the subsequent sequence of actions are stored in electrical bobbins. These will in turn control the many relays. The number of holes to be punched at one time must be less than fifty percent of the 960 possible. Because the pressure needed to punch more would be so heavy that the whole 'Mixer' would promptly fall through the floor.

He asked the instructor: "What is this 'thing' in the data processing world used for?" The teacher wrestled for an answer. Apparently, in vain because an explanation did not come.

The other future BULL technicians in his class didn't seem to care. The purpose of this device is somehow, at least until today, mysterious. But he would have liked to know it. The other 'trainees' didn't seem to care. They are probably already in their thoughts at the first long-awaited extended home leave weekend.

And now something exceptional happened again. And again after a completed 'phase' of the training! The last Friday before the weekend 'break' he wanted, as it is customary in France, to shake hands with the teacher. The man waved him aside and asked: "Do you have a moment?" Superfluous question. You always have to have time for a supervisor. He pulled him back and whispered: "But it is top secret!!! Actually, nobody knows the practical use of the 'Mixer'. Its developer has left the company. Now it is only used to duplicate punched cards".

So far, only the creating, sorting, and manipulating of punched cards were explained. No mentioning of processing the data like calculation of hopefully useful results and printing those on paper.

The next device he was learning did this. The so-called 'Tabulator' is also making a disagreeable noise. The whole, again a 'Monster', is about two meters long, one meter wide, and about 120 centimeters high. The relays which control the device are located in again very solidly built cabinets. Covered with the familiar ugly iron sheet metal. The relays are ten centimeters high with an electrical coil of 2 centimes in diameter. When the relay is activated, then the electrical contacts on the top of it close or open. There are up to 12 such contacts. They are made of tungsten. A not cheap, hard metal with high conductivity and not susceptible to the inevitable erosion.

The maintenance requires regular cleaning of the contacts of the relays with a brush equipped with steel wires. Must be done carefully and with great sensitivity. The risk of bending the contacts is very high.

Then the closing time of those must be measured and checked. It must be less than a millisecond. This time is extremely important for the correct functioning of the tabulator and, like everything in a computer, must be adhered to very precisely.

The mechanical-electrical calculating units are on the surface of the device. Up to twelve according to what the customer had the need or was willing to pay for. The units which perform the arithmetic calculations are constructed with mechanical components and electrical magnetic coils. The gearwheels in there are driven by an electric motor. The number of revolutions of this motor must again be very precise. The regulation is done like this: Outside on the axis of the motor is a disc with regularly painted white stripes on its outer edge. Using an exactly oscillating tuning fork, the maintenance technician must see an uninterrupted white band through the small slits at their top. Then the speed is right. If not, then it must be adjusted by changing the supply voltage of the motor. At the top, in the middle, there is the printing output device. A printer again equipped with rotating discs. The bills, account statements, order list, and their likes are then printed on an 'endless' paper. This paper has small holes on its sides. Through those, the paper is moved over with ink saturated ribbon. The symbols on the rotating discs were exactly in the millisecond when they appeared above the stamp and then printed. These 'hammers' are activated by a strong electromagnet.

After a roll of paper is used up, a new one has to be mounted. Fortunately, the replacement of a used-up paper roll is the duty of the operating personnel and not of the technician. A procedure that often has driven the female operator to despair. But the maintenance staff had the much more unpleasant task to install a fresh black ribbon. With the risk of again having the white nylon shirt sprayed with black ink. Also, the same risk as with the already described 'Traducteuse'.

The steering and control of the to be carried out functions are accomplished by a 'program'. In the tabulator, a program is done in the following way: On one side of the tabulator, there is an easily removable plateau. About twenty by fifty centimeters in size and three centimeters thick. It can be unhooked with one hand. The programmer has to do this to create or better to 'wire' a program. This plateau is equipped with holes. In a matrix of 10 per row and 30 rows. In these 'plugs' small gray cables are inserted. On the right vertical are the plugs which distribute the so-called clock impulses. Those are generated by the motor which had to have, as said, the very exact number of revolutions.

The execution of the program was now accomplished as follows: The impulses are fed by the small cables into one of the other sockets to the left of the ones who distribute the clock pulses. The copper wires which are soldered behind those sockets lead to the relays, the coils of the computing units, and the magnets of the printer.

He understood it immediately. And it was fun to 'wire up' such a program himself. Well understood, manually plugging cables. And not like in the mechanical booking machines, clipping little metal pieces. Typing a program online with a keyboard into a computer, as is done today, was still decades away. This primitive method to 'build' a program also has its pitfalls. He later had to experience this himself.

24. Tabulator　　　　　**25. Calculating Unit**

2.6. The BULL Gama 3

Back to classrooms in Paris. The 'education' to become a completely qualified maintenance technician is far from over. Now, a very different kind and a more modern device was in the training program. Back then, the name 'computer' was still not a general term. That is probably the name for one of these modern 'von Neumann' machines. Such a thing is now entering his life. And from now on, these 'real' computers will shape his future...

First, the famous tube calculator BULL Gamma 3.
The at that time director of the company BULL, Pierre Letort, described in the magazine 'Arts et Manufacture' No. 22 of June 1953 the operation of the Gamma 3 as follows:
In its current form, the electronic computer works as an additional device for the punched-card machines to which it is connected. The punched card machine senses the cards inserted in the feed magazine and sends the read values to the electronic computer, from which it, in turn, receives the results, which it writes or punches depending on the way it works. But what calculation may also be provided, the result of the electron computer is created as quickly that it seems to be timeless.

42

The fully expanded Gamma 3 has 7 run-time memories with a capacity of 12 decimal places each, which are divided into a calculation memory and 6 number memories. They are located in so-called 'storage cabinets' with 24 storage units for each 12 decimal places. So, the space requirement is that of a wardrobe to store 24 twelve-digit decimal numbers!!!

Overall, the computer is equipped with almost 400 electron tubes. The electron computer is adapted to the slow punched card machine by means of electron tubes which temporarily store the binary states.

A very precise technical description. Most likely not written by the before mentioned gentleman. After all, he was the CEO (Chief Executive Officer). But the engineers he hired who created this 'computer' were very capable.

So, this technical sensation at that time has to be mastered now. Will he ever have to repair them?

As is well known by now, he loves such difficult tasks. And there is no risk of a dirty shirt. Electrons do not make any noise and do not cause ink splashes.

But even with the 'miracle thing' there were also many mechanical parts involved. It was the framework, which in turn consists of the well-known ugly gray iron sheet metal. The fold-out chassis are equipped with the required electronic components. These are located on one side of the large, very heavy cabinet, measuring two by two meters.

Then, there was the need for the massive plug, weighing ten kilograms, to connect to one of the punched card machines. The plug is equipped with up to a hundred wires. Every one of those in their own color combination. The entire cable is a thick gray hose that is reminiscent of a boa. And extremely dangerous. The risk of tripping over it is great.

And the SUVA (Schweizerische Unfall Versicherungs Anstalt = Swiss Professional Accident Insurance) did not even protest. Half of the ugly 'block' contained the elements of the power supply. Eight different voltages were required. 6-volt direct current for heating the filaments of the tubes. 200 volt direct current for their anode voltage. Then 20 volts DC for the relays used in the device. Then alternating current for the motors of the fans, which have to blow away the heat caused by the tubes.

The rectification from alternating current to direct current is accomplished by a series of selenium plates. They measure ten by ten centimeters and are three millimeters thick. They are huge, large and assembled in series for the required performance. Selenium is a metal that only allows the current to pass in one direction. Such rectifiers were used before the rectifier tubes and the much later developed semiconductors The tiny amounts of binary data were temporarily stored this way: On the fold-out chassis, there are electrical coils and capacitors connected in series. This combination delays the electric impulses is also called 'delay line'. The impulses are switched from the output of the combination back to their input. The binary data rotates in a circle. This is equivalent to storing them. The signals must be amplified between the coils and the capacitors. This is achieved through the interposition of electronic tubes, the 'Triode'. In these radio tubes is the current between the anode (positive pole) and cathode (negative pole) controlled by a grid in between. To enable the current through the vacuum, the cathode pole must be heated with a filament. This is a wire comparable with the one in an incandescent lamp, which is made to glow by the 6-volt direct current just mentioned.

The maintenance of the BULL Gamma 3 consists of checking the tension and temperature in the 'box' and testing the filament of the electronic tubes. This filament is the most vulnerable element in a Gamma 3. It had an average lifetime of 10 years. In order to prevent a failure of the 'electronic brain', this filament has to be 'stressed' every day. This is how it was done: A program written specifically for this purpose was run on the machine. With the use of a small rubber hammer, the tops of the electronic tubes were hit with a slight 'touch'. And this on four hundred of them! If the test program does not show any failure, the tube is still in order. Otherwise, it has to be replaced immediately.

He enjoys making the 'hammer man'. Much easier and less manual heavy work than with the 'apparatuses' that he has been learned up to now. Those now seemed to him completely outdated!

- **26. BULL Gamma 3**

- **27. Gamma 3 Frame**

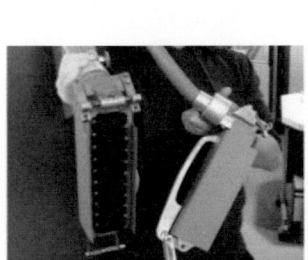

- **28. Gamma 3 Cable.**

29. Electronic Tube ECC83

2.7. The 'real' live with the machines from BULL.

That was it for Paris! The 'training' is over. It wasn't always a pleasure. The pretty girl which killed the card-puncher was the most exciting experience.

Quote: "What doesn't kill me makes me stronger". (Frederic Nietzsche).

It didn't kill him. He was not sent home either. How the results of the weekly written and practical tests turned out is beyond his knowledge. His feeling about the results is not too bad. Most of the time he was done before the others. Without being bathed in sweat like some of his Swiss colleagues. The Swedes seemed to have taken the matter more lightly. Definitely a lot 'cooler'. After all, they are from the north...

Back in Zurich. Now he had to apply what he learned. Had to prove to the company that their investment had paid off. At first, it was fun. He was accompanied by an experienced senior technician on the 'missions' at the customer's location. Also, this time, he was not thrown alone into the famous cold water.

But like so often with him: If something becomes a habit, it's soon getting boring.

Nevertheless, he was often challenged more than he liked. As by now is well known: He needs those. Not the tiring routine maintenance work. This caused, as is also well known, dirty hands and a dirty shirt

But there were also positive experiences. For example, the admiring look at him from the director of the in those days, very prestigious, shoe dealer group. This man, the coincidence wanted it, was on the spot when he was called up the same day because of a breakdown of their tabulator. The top boss personally checked periodically the performance of his so expensively paid machines.

He falsely proudly calls them: 'Electron brains'. And was very sure of his statement. The expression of 'brain' is much exaggerated. The customer apparently could not afford the Gamma 3. Despite the ever-increasing sales figures. Or it was not needed for the creation of the mostly smaller invoices.

Does he deserve the look of acknowledgment from the 'chief'? Yes! He had the problem immediately under control. After a breakdown in the city's electricity grid, the motor of the tabulator no longer turns with the exact number of revolutions.

Another also very critical customer was a wholesale company. The delivery papers must have been completed every morning before 8 a.m. The drivers of half a dozen heavy trucks were waiting impatiently for those.
So, woe we, if a punched card processing device failed at night.
A standby service was specially organized for this customer. So, he had to expect to be woken up by a nerving, noisy phone call shortly after midnight.
This happened only once. Nothing was damaged. That he could hear in the voice of the lady who called. She simply did not succeed in installing a new paper roll. Sometimes women are a bit helpless when exposed to higher technology (sorry ladies...). Or she was just bored. He was not even angry with her. She was beautifully well-dressed and therefore also very sexy.
Also in the next episode were women closely involved. One like a witch with a broom. The other one was a good fairy.
The case took place in Lugano in southern Switzerland. At the time between Christmas and New Year. It was the time of the annual final financial calculations.
The customer was a very well-known major Swiss bank. At that time, it still had the word 'Anstalt' (German for 'Institution') in the company name. He was ordered to be present and to be immediately ready to act in the case of a failure.
Such ones were quite predictable.
The work environment or rather the place he had to wait to be useful was rather friendly. To his pleasure, the staff there was mostly female and pretty. And dressed in skirts and white blouses, as was in those days the norm.
They mostly spoke Swiss German. Only the cleaning lady was Italian. She lived most likely in nearby Italy and passes daily the border to earn a lot more money than in her country.
She only appeared after midnight. He never met her. That is why he cannot say whether she was pretty and how she was

dressed. But she worked very thoroughly. He soon found that out.

And it was very terrifying!

One morning there was total panic in the 'shop'. The main program no longer worked properly. The results produced by the tabulator were wrong in the order of millions of Swiss francs.

Highest alarm level! Extremely urgent 'firefighter' mission for him.

The bank's head office in Zurich was immediately informed. This promptly triggered a phone call to the director of BULL Switzerland. The man was still titled 'Director' and not yet CEO. The boss of the bank had to show his counterpart how furious he was.

With full concentration, although not yet fully awake, he went to work. As usual in such a case. The learned controls gave no explanation. He held his head down and walked almost like in a bad dream around in circles, staring desperately at the floor. And what did he see there?

Wonderful enlightenment!

Probably thanks to his almost proverbial intuition. On the side where the panel with the 'program' is mounted one end of these, for the program needed, gray small cables hung loose in the air.

Sabotage?

No: The cleaning lady! As it turned out later, her broom had with heavy momentum accidentally torn the cable out of the socket!

The problem was recognized. But not solved yet. Because he didn't know in which hole he has to put the detached cable.

This was a case for the programmer. And the man is in Zurich. But he was not even there. The man was on vacation in the Bahamas.

His fury and frustration hit the ceiling. Vacation? And this at the time of the annual final calculation!

He stood there, almost like the famous donkey on the mountain!!! (German expression for total helplessness).

But wonder happen!

Or better. It was the idea of a very intelligent woman who had immediately realized the disastrous situation.
She said without any emotions: "The programmer has documented his program very precisely. The documents are secretly stored in the main safe in the bank".
They were there! Within a very short time, the cable was anchored in the right place and the spook was over.

Just to be replaced by another soon.

In the form of light gray smoke that dared to rise above one of the calculating units on top of the tabulator. A very alarming smell was creeping out.
This time the problem was immediately recognized as such. The solution to it, however, was much more difficult. And, above all, much more time-consuming than the one which was caused by the cleaning woman's broom.
Because the so urgently needed calculating unit was not included in the local spare set. For cost reasons?
But now, whatever it will cost, a new unit must be installed as soon as possible.
Another, even more angry, phone call with the headquarters in Zurich.
At that time, callable courier service did not yet exist. So, the replacement must be otherwise delivered. This was now organized in a flash. A chauffeur was soon on the move. At that time, there were fortunately not so many traffic jams on the north side of the Gotthard.
The professional driver for the 'chiefs' came with the special limousine of the general manager, a Citroën CS19. The most modern car in the world at that time. Luckily, the car was not in the repair shop, as was so often the case. The car was very speedy, so in almost no time the badly needed part was in Lugano.

The job with BULL had, after a short while, lost its attractiveness. It was becoming more boring every day and did no longer challenge his brain.

Unfortunately, no Gamma 3 had up to today been sold in all of Switzerland. Their maintenance would have placed a higher demand on the intellect.

But now he thinks like this: "It was probably better that he did not have the opportunity to prove his capacity to solve complicated problems. With 400 hundred electron tubes whose filaments have an average lifespan of ten years. This will result in a failure rate of the device in the range of lousy 9 days".

This lousy meantime between breakdowns was even for him frustrating.

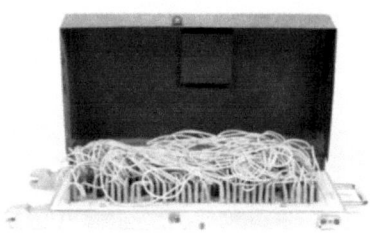

• **30. BULL Tabulator Program Board**

3. The Start of a very great time. (1964)

3.1. The unbelievable 'story' of his start with CDC.

The BULL Gamma 3 was an electronic tube calculator. To call it a 'computer' is this not a bit exaggerated? It was a step in the long evolution of the 'von Neumann' machines. A certain Karl Zuse created a sensational one. He was one of the first real pioneers of what probably nobody ever imagined themselves at the time: The incredible, awesome development of what has driven history of humans into an entirely new dimension.
For him, at the end of 1963, a whole new life began. And at first, he had no idea what will come at him.

His experiences so far with the 'matter' seemed to be what he was learning in the first grade of primary school. So to speak: In the ancient world of computer science. Or, at least, it seemed that until now, only early Middle Age was reached.
He was tired of the daily, almost boring work. Had no fun anymore with the machines from BULL. The work with them became monotonous. There were fewer and fewer of those famous and needed challenges. And as it looked, a Gamma 3 cannot be sold in Switzerland. Let alone in Zurich. And he was still quite young. Even when he often appeared to be old. Especially when his troubleshooting was not accomplished in the desired time.

Something new had to be found. And with BULL, there was nothing in sight. It was only when the company later merged with Honeywell and became Honeywell-Bull that there were drastic changes coming. But Honeywell brought in the 'pepper', the modern computers. The mechanical equipment which handled the punched cards was brought in by BULL and then incorporated in the joint venture.
He had not to go through the merger. He left BULL before. Not truly thankful to the company which, at least, enabled him to start his professional career. And also paid for.

51

Huge happiness suddenly happened. The opportunity which so surprisingly arrived was too irresistible to not be taken. What 'wonder' was this?

The Control Data Corporation, the CDC.

The job advertisement in the newspaper by this American company, which was completely unknown to him and almost all non-specialists, stated something like this: We are looking for technicians for our supercomputer CDC 6600 just sold to CERN (Center European de Recherche Nucléaire) in Geneva. Computer experience, good English skills, and the willingness to get trained in the USA and then to work in Meyrin GE were the requirements they asked for.

By the way, the entire 'deal' had brought CDC, as he heard much later, over eight million. In 1963 in the fairly hard Swiss Francs.

He hardly believes that he could get such an attractive job. Lack of relevant experience with transistor computers. But who had them back then? And with his rudimentary English learned in evening courses in a private language school
.

Quote: "He who risks nothing wins nothing".

He immediately called the Zurich office of CDC Switzerland. A gentleman who spoke Swiss German was on the phone and introduces himself: "I am the chief secretary and also for the time the director of CDC Switzerland". As it turned out later, the whole Swiss subsidiary consisted only of the boss, three secretaries, two programmers, and a technician.

The gentleman invited him for an interview. This will take place in only two days. The engineer from Minneapolis, responsible for the hiring, will only be here for a very short time. They apparently were under terrible pressure. Courses begin in Minnesota in March. It was already late November!

For such an opportunity, he will drop all others of his activities. So, he immediately accepted the day and the time of the interview.

The gentleman was pleased: "Good. And send us for a

recruitment usually needed document per express mail to the Zurich address. I will translate them to English. The manager from Minneapolis doesn't speak a word of German".

Speaking German is not to be expected from a Midwestern American. But first, he had to search on a map where Minneapolis and Minnesota are located. It is west of the Mississippi. The state borders on its northern side to Canada. Then the interview took place. He was quite a bit more than only just nervous when waiting in the reception room in the chic office in an expensive building near the Paradeplatz in Zurich.

There were computer magazines in English on a small glass table in the waiting room. He loosely leafed through them. He understood almost nothing. But what he learned was that this machine, the CDC 6600, was admired and praised everywhere. As the most modern, the leading, and the most powerful of what has been brought onto the market so far. Sounds already very promising! But is he the man for it?

Will see!

He had to wait endless long minutes. Another candidate was in at the interview.

Meanwhile, the secretary chatted with him in a friendly manner and did not even ask specific questions. The door opened. The other applicant said: "Goodbye". In accent-free Oxford English.

A plump, jovial medieval gentleman now greeted him in the broadest 'Yankee slang'. The man was not dressed in a suit like him. But in jeans, sneakers and a gray T-shirt which had with big letters 'CDC' written on the back. The Chief engineer sat opposite him at an elegant meeting table. The 'Ami' started slowly to talk to him. The interviewer looked at him quite incomprehensibly. He had probably asked a question and was waiting for an answer. He, the job applicant, answered from now on. Less with words, but with gestures of affirmation or negation. Depending on the expressions that flit across the face of the man who vividly reminded him of a cowboy.

53

After half an hour, he was relieved from the painful 'procedure'. He wanted now to shake hands with the engineer. The man stared at him with astonishment. Apparently, shaking hands is not so common in the Midwest.

The secretary seemed to have impatiently waited for the end of the interview because he immediately came to him and asked "How did it go? Are you employed?" He lied: "It went ..." Now he was very, very embarrassed. Definitely visible to his counterpart. And whispered, extremely ashamed: "You have to ask the gentleman from Minneapolis". The secretary then did so. Also in Swiss German colored English and certainly not in the US jargon. To his great astonishment, the 'cowboy' nodded. And mumbled something like: "Mister Fischer is responsible for details of the contract such as wage, training and so on". Then the apparently very hungry man went to the door with a sturdy step and asked: "Where's the nearest MacDonald?"

The unexpected finale came now. The secretary said: "You got the job! Employment begins on March 1st. We'll talk about everything else later".

Everything else didn't matter to him now. It will be fine for sure. But what came now had to come! Mr. Fischer said, yes, he almost shouted: "But now English has to be learned with full concentration!!!" That was an extremely strict Swiss military command tone.

Now the first action to be done was to cancel his work contract with BULL. He didn't even think that leaving BULL could cause serious difficulties. The employment contract contained a clause that specifies that the employee is not allowed to work for a competitor for 3 years after the dismissal. This clause he would, if needed, encounter with: "CDC is not a competitor. They are technically too far ahead".

The first day with CDC arrived. It was a day of sitting around. He was there exactly on time, 0830. At around nine, an elegant dressed lady in a pleated skirt and cleanly polished black shoes with high heels appeared. She looked at him in astonishment. But then, as they say in Zurich, the twenty-cent coin fell. She asked: "Are you the new employee for the 6600 in Geneva?" Yes, he is. She looked at him with a smile and with a certain admiration. She explained to him that the temporary chief is not here today because he is at CERN. In Zurich, there will not be an office for him. He will not work here anyway. Then she said very firmly: "You must first fill in this form for the American embassy in Bern. Because you need a visa as soon as possible. The training begins as discussed on March 15th in Minneapolis".

Luckily, he had his passport and others for the visa application essential papers with him. And a dictionary. He was busy for over an hour completing the form. Not without sweating and swearing.

The lady must have seen this. She asked: "Do you want a coffee?".

Of course, he wants one after the stress of filling out the request for a visa. He replied: "An espresso if possible". The coffee was immediately, elegantly served on a plateau. Then she pushed at him a large stack of booklets, improvised drawings (blueprints) with completely unintelligible symbols, and loose sheets with hand-scribbled diagrams. He should go through this 'stuff' today and then take them home.

31. CDC 6600

3.2. The CDC 1604 at ETH (1964).

Then the lady said: "On Wednesday, March 3rd, you are ordered to help to install a CDC 1604 at the ETH in Zurich". He didn't even know that there exists such a machine. So, he went ahead and 'dived' into the literature. He was so busy with it that he did not notice the arrival of two other ladies, They were equally dressed as the first one. A gentleman also arrived. He introduced himself in pure Zurich dialect and with the typical accent spoken in the western slum of the city: "I am Edi". The man said that he is his future colleague and that he has employee number 7 in CDC Switzerland. Therefore, logically, the new one, namely him, will get the number 8. He was number 8 throughout the 17 years he was with CDC. In 1981, there were more than one hundred and twenty employees in Switzerland alone. At the zenith of the CDC when it was number 3 worldwide in the 'computer business' there were about 50000 'heads' employed by the company.

The CDC 1604 was the first computer using transistors at the ETH (Eidgenösische Technische Hochschule = Federal Institute of Technology). Previously, they had a Zuse Z4 installed. This machine was found after World War 2 in a barn in southern Germany by an at that time very progressively thinking professor. The ETH rebuilt the electronic tube calculator. Later, the ETH designed and builds its own one, the ERMETH (Elektronische Rechenmaschine ETH=Electronic Calculating Machine ETH).
This professor often tried desperately to mobilize the Swiss machine industry to produce also something like this, or even better and more modern. Switzerland was indeed thanks to their highly developed technique of precision mechanics and leading in manufacturing of electrical equipment ready to have success in building peripheral devices for computers or even computers themselves. The professor wasted his time. Probably because the Swiss industrialists and the credit giving banks stuck to the motto of the famous Swiss Philosopher Nicklaus von der Flüeh: "Do not make the frontier too wide". ETH had the courage and the money to buy a CDC 1604. The name of the machine was, for everybody, astonishing. Where

does it come from? This name was one of Seymore Cray's most guarded secrets. Was it because It was developed by Seymour and his crew at Park Avenue No. 1604 in downtown Minneapolis? There are other 'versions' and 'rumors' floating around that try to clear the source of the mysterious number 1604. A name very disliked by CDC's marketing managers. The CDC 160-A was also manufactured there. This computer was also designed by Seymour Cray. During a short three-day stay in a hospital. This he was told later in Minneapolis. It served the 1604 as a front-end processor to control the so-called peripheral devices such as card readers, printers, magnetic band stations, and disk storage units. The computer from IBM and others had at that time employed the complicated 'interrupt' procedure, which interrupts the current user program when the system needs the processor to control the peripheral devices.

32. Konrad Zuse (1910-1995)
Computer Pioneer

33. Seymour Cray (1925-1996)
The 'father' of Supercomputers

34. CDC 1604

35. CDC 160-A

4. Minnepolis, Minnesota. (1964)

4.1. The first days in Minneapolis

Minneapolis, here I come..

.

On March 13th, 1964, the Swissair flight number 100 from Zurich to New York had him on board. After arriving, he had to struggle through US entry control. With more than just a critical eye from the controlling officer. But his business visa B4 apparently calmed him. Then the passing through the customs control. His only suitcase was not even opened but immediately thrown to the grim-looking black muscled baggage porter behind the entrance control.
The trip continued with Northwest Orient Airline.
The airplane was half empty. Therefore, the extremely friendly, smiling stewardesses. Dressed in the colors of the airline: Blue-yellow and still wearing skirts. A can of Coca-Cola and a reasonably eatable sandwich were for free. Of course, only in a cardboard cup and without a plate. He did not care. He was already dead tired. He almost missed the approach to the airfield of the 'Twin City' Minneapolis-St. Paul Airport.
He was shaken briskly by the roar of the winter storm outside. The landing made him more than only slightly trembling. The pilot needed three approaches to get the airplane onto the ground.
With still fragile legs he was picked up by a fat, always laughing, jovial gentleman and immediately driven to the hotel in the center of the city. The man said something like he is responsible for the 'trainees' from Europe. The gentleman said: "I will guide you to the training center on Monday". At least that's what he thought to have understood. Or better what he guessed. Good night! There will be a great problem to learn this rudimentary American English, which they are speaking here.

It was Sunday in Minneapolis in early March. He was in a totally different world than he was used to and which he had naively not imagined like this. Sunday morning. Well-rested? A good dose of jet lag was certainly still latent. But at that time, he didn't even know what that is.

His first American breakfast. In a second-class business hotel. The breakfast was also strange to him: Fried eggs, hash browns potatoes, and half-burned slices of bread with salted butter. Served with lousy very hot liquid black stuff which must be coffee. As much as you wanted. The waitress ran around with the bullet-shaped jug and refilled the big cup on his table. Not even asking if he wants this.

But the weather was nice. Great for a little tour in the city. There will surely be a nice avenue along the Mississippi with restaurants and chic shops. Just like the Limmatquai in Zurich. It was uncomfortably cold outside. The streets were deserted. Similar to the charming painting from Edward Hopper titled 'Early Sunday Morning' which he loves so much. Only here he was not in a small town in the East of America, but in a metropolis in the Midwest. With gray painted, desolate skyscrapers on both sides of the straight streets with exact right-angled intersections. Without cars.
The river was very far away. On the map which he already got in Zurich, everything looked much closer. There was no sidewalk on the very broad bridge he reached after about half an hour of fast walking. So, he had to stay on this side of the Mississippi. The river, deep underneath the bridge, looked to him like a frozen trickle.
No open shops. Let alone a restaurant. And he was freezing, too. Only later, back at the hotel, he did realize that the temperature was ten Celsius degrees below zero. He had to calculate this with his luckily still existing school knowledge. The thermometer on the outside of the hotel shows the temperature, of course, only in Fahrenheit.

Monday was the first day of school.
The first part of the theoretical training, which lasted three weeks, started.
The female instructor's welcome speech was rather cool and without a handshake. The other 'trainees' were all Americans. From different states. He heard this from the lively discussions

they had before the beginning of the class. This in spite of his more than only basic and very incomplete English.

For the next weeks, language was his biggest problem. In the more prestigious private language schools, such as the one he went through, one learns to ask: "Where can I park my Rolls-Royce?" But not how to order a hamburger in Minneapolis.

At first, there was no mention of hardware. They had first to learn to program. Already the next day they were obliged to write a small program. In the programming language FORTRAN (Formula Translation). FORTRAN was one of the first higher-level programming languages. Of course: Invented by IBM.
There was no computer in the hotel, but a card-puncher. The punched cards were then sent to the computing center in the headquarters and the results are delivered the next day.
His first program of ten FORTRAN statements resulted in ten FORTRAN errors! A bitter disappointment! He was so firmly convinced that he had understood and implemented everything correctly.

More than to 'fight' with computer languages was to learn the 'unreal' English used here. He immediately began to write down the most commonly used words and expressions. Then, after work, he tries to find their meaning in German in his extra-large American-oriented dictionary. Memorizing them was another big challenge. A cheap radio receiver was purchased at a used stuff dealer and switched on whenever possible. To write again the unknown expressions down. They had to be processed by his brain. And this a.s.a.p.

After three weeks, as announced, the practical training began. This was now taking place in the factory in Bloomington, a western suburb of Minneapolis. The company's headquarters was also located there. The suburb is about 10 miles, more than 16 kilometers, away from the city center.
To commute between downtown and Bloomington, a car will be provided for him. No question about a valid driver's license. Of course, it was assumed that he had such a one. In

61

Switzerland, he was 'only' allowed to drive a motorcycle, and he had the permission to learn to drive a car. He only had a few hours of driving practice with the shaky Volkswagen of his apprenticeship colleague.

He kept this fact of not having a driver's license in silence. He wanted to avoid being 'shipped' back to Zurich immediately. The car was ready for him next Friday evening. The car key was handed to him without any questions.

Most of the cars had left the huge parking area. So, he found 'his' car immediately, an older Ford. Luckily, not a Cadillac with a gigantic tail fin. The modest Ford was therefore much easier to manipulate. It was now time for him to drive around a few rounds in the immense, empty parking lot. Then he activated all the possible courage and 'trembled' home. In the now very little traffic and luckily broad, wide streets. A long search for a large parking lot. followed.

Intensive personal driving school on Saturday and Sunday was needed.

And it worked without too much-unwanted strangling of the motor.

On the coming Monday morning, he had to get up very, very early. Before the usual morning traffic rush, he had to be in Bloomington!

4.2. Living next door to Alice.

He now rented a small and very poorly furnished 'studio' in a shabby brick building located just at the border of a slum. The building contained only one-room apartments. But very cheap. On the same level lived a little young lady. It turned out later that she was from Finland.

The lady's flat was just next door to his. Like in the so beautiful and praised song and popular pop hit "Living next door to Alice". Is it not also her first name? She was for women coming from Northern Europe atypically small, atypically insecure, and atypically very nervous. There are a lot of Scandinavians who immigrated to Minnesota. Clear, the climate, the flora, the fauna, and the many lakes are very

similar to those in Northern Europe.
She spoke very little. The first time they talked to each other was in the hotel 'Normandy Village'. This was a popular meeting place for the city's 'singles' on Saturday evenings. With a 'piano bar'. There you sit, female and male, around a large concert piano. The pianist plays popular folk songs. Those who can sing or have drunken enough sing along. The Budweiser beer, which was very expensive for him, did not really taste good. But it costs a whopping 80 cents and had to be paid immediately in cash. Compare this to the fact that a gallon of petrol at that time cost 'lousy 18 cents!.
The beer was usually consumed standing up. The places to sit around the piano were reserved for regular guests. So, not for him

He felt lonely in this place.

And he was soon also already a bit 'messed' up.
Until he saw something, which immediately woke him up: The lady from next door!
Very nicely dressed, white blouse, black skirt, fishnet stockings, and high-heels.

It almost took his breath away.

Her steps fluctuated slightly. But she recognized him. Scandinavians are generally not so used to alcohol. He experienced that himself in Sweden. He dared to speak to her. In Swedish. Finns understand this very often. She answered in more than just broken English. And of course, she immediately asked: "Where are you from?" To his astonishment, she knew where Switzerland is. Not like so many of those living here in the Midwest. For them, 'Switzerland' and 'Sweden' are about the same. Her second question was, also as usual, at the beginning of a flirt: "What are you doing here?" He replied: "I work with computers". In a kind of admiring look at him and getting somewhat gently blushing. She says predicatively:

"Ah, with these IBM machines?"

"No, with Control Data"

First, she looked like a question mark. Then it seemed that she had realized what he said, then the answer came skillfully: "I always also look at the expiry date of a product that I buy"

An entirely different kind of 'Data'.

Very, very, unfortunately, the beginning of a possible, beautiful, and long overdue 'love story' no longer continued. The 'affair' stopped for him far too early.

4.3. The Card-Reader, Printer, and Tape stations.

It is not the fabulous 6600 that is being instructed first. As it should be, the training was started with the so-called peripheral devices. Until now, he had only vaguely heard of this term. It was not used so often by the French. He already knows machines that read cards. The one from CDC was much more advanced than those from BULL. The cards are no longer mechanically pushed forward. The feeding of the cards into the reader is made by a system with a rapidly rotating drum, measuring ten centimeters in diameter. The cards are sucked through small holes with a vacuum pump and 'hunted' through the electronic reading station. The loading area and the receiving box are also much longer than those at BULL. They are more than one meter in length. Sufficiently long for most of the read in programs which were punched on cards. These programs were written in eider FORTRAN or COMPASS. Compass was the ASSEMBLER language used for the CDC 6000 series.
The second device to be learned is the line printer. Also, much more modern than the printers on the BULL tabulators. And also, of course, much more expensive. The letters were no longer etched on individual disks, but on a large shaft made of stainless steel. It is 80 centimeters long and 8 centimeters in

diameter. This shaft in turn rotates at high speed. Below is the to be printed paper. It is fed over a wide with black ink saturated ribbon. Very strong magnets then release a spring, which hammers a lever against the paper with great force. And this in the millisecond when the character to be printed is exactly there. It exists an exceptional 'story' about these springs. They were made from a special steel alloy that was developed for Swiss machine guns before the Second World War. The instructor whispers this to him. In reasonably passable US English.
Please note: This alloy was one of the most strictly guarded secrets of the Swiss armament industry before and during the Second World War.

The training continued. Next came the magnetic tape stations. There were two different models for the CDC 6600 series computer, The CDC 606 for the commonly used 12.2 mm. (1/2 inch) wide tapes for 6-bit words (frames) per a half millimeter of the tape. The second, the CDC 626, was special. It used tapes with a width of 25.4 millimeters (1 inch) and 12-Bit words. Each of the devices has two ten centimeters wide and one meter deep 'shafts' on the front. The magnetic tape is 'sucked' into these 'shafts' by vacuum pumps. This is to avoid that the tape tears apart when the movement is briskly stopped.
The CDC 626, as it clearly turned out later, was a catastrophic 'flop' that did not last long. The problem is as follows:
The magnetic tape reels required are quite heavy.
The fourteen (12 data, 2 parity bits) reading diodes must be aligned very precisely. At the time, this was almost impossible to be achieved mechanically. To read the 14 bits in the right order, electrical adjustments must be done. This was achieved by adapting the electrical resistance in the wires between the sensors and the receiving electronic. The adjusting to achieve the correct result was done by adjusting the time a signal takes between the write-read heads and the receivers mounted in the chassis. Later, at CERN, he was for hours, days, and weeks suffering to make these adjustments.

Again later, Visitors, especially technical laypeople, heavily admired the magnetic tape stations. At least you could see something which is moving and could even hear a considerable noise.

36. CDC 606 Tape Station

37. CDC 405 Card Reader

3

38. CDC Line Printer

4.4. The famous disc storage unit CDC 6603.

The next and last one of the peripheral devices was the Disc Storage Unit. Seymour Cray once said to him: "This is our best piece". This, of course, did not correspond to the facts. The best was definitely Seymour Cray's 6600. At least that's the opinion of the little Swiss 'apprentice sorcerer'.
The 'wonder device', the most fascinating of all up to that time sold disc storage drives, was manufactured by a company called Bryant in Detroit. Please note, by German toolmakers.

As he was often told with high respect. The highest precision was extremely necessary. The arms with the reading heads are brought into the correct position hydraulically with oil pressure. They have to be in the exactness of a fraction of a millimeter in the correct position. And this within 3 milliseconds. The program which reads the data does this just after it issued the 'positioning' order. It does not wait for the heads to be in position. When the data is read without a parity error, then it is assumed that the heads are at their place. This verification was possible thanks to the help of the parity bit attached to each byte. In 'normal' disc storage units, the driver program would wait a predefined time in order to be sure that the heads are in place, Not so in the CDC 6603. There, every microsecond saved in such a 'complex' system is worth money.

Have you got that? Haben Sie es verstanden?_Vous l'avez? Ce l'hai fatta?_¿Entendiste eso? Har du förtaat?

The entire device, despite being made of aluminum, weighs a thousand kilos. During the process of positioning the write-read heads, when they are 'pressed' 30 centimeters from one extreme position to the other, the whole machine 'jumps' noticeably. Therefore, despite its weight, it has to be firmly anchored on the double floor of the computer room. To place filled coffee cups on top of it is strictly forbidden. There is a high danger that the coffee will soon not be in the cup anymore.
The device is of a very bulky appearance because the rotating 14 plates are about 120 cm in diameter and made from a magnesium alloy. About a centimeter thick and mounted on a huge steel shaft. These plates were very popular with the 'engineers' like him when the device was no longer in use. This was, of course, several years later. The disks served as tabletops for garden tables, which therefore became very exquisite. The magnesium discs should, in fact, be burned. This was requested by the American nuclear research institutes. So that no information could get to Russia. Nevertheless, maintenance requires that all 'magnetic' bits on the disk be erased once a week. This happened with a long

fork that was pushed between them as the plates rotated. A strong permanent magnet was attached to the front of the fork. The instrument got the nickname 'Candy Cane'.

This device is extremely expensive, in the order of more than0000 USD, disk storage unit CDC 6603 could maximum 10store about 300 megabytes. Today, a 12-centimeter CD has a capacity of more than 700 megabytes and costs about one Swiss franc.

40. CDC 6603 Disc Drive

4.5. Car 'stories'.

After three weeks with plenty of practical hands-on exercises on the learned devices and many late evening driving back to downtown, he was ready for the car driving test! Fortunately, this also took place in Bloomington. The theory test was rather simple. The answer did not have to be formulated, they only had to be marked on a prepared sheet. The driving took place in a closed area without any other traffic. Some not even narrow curves had to be 'mastered.' Then he had to stop and restart on a hill which is not too steep for Swiss standards. This was followed by short backward parking in a huge parking space. No questions or chatting while driving. The only

commands were: "Straight, Right, Left".
But suddenly a brusque command was shouted at him: "Stop!"
The hydraulic brakes worked fine. Both men were almost
flying through the windshield.
The 'tester' did critically observe this: One hand on the
steering wheel, the other manipulating the direction indicator.
Then the movement of the head in front of an intersection.
There are not many of them, and no crossing vehicles were to
be expected. But the explicit look to the left and right had to be
checked. Then the readiness to be always able to activate the
break with the left foot is also closely observed. How to handle
the handbrake was tested too. He never used them. It is
almost everywhere flat in the Midwest. Inserting the gear lever
into 'P' is sufficient.
The expert became very friendly: "Ah, from Switzerland? Do
you ski?" No, he doesn't. And he doesn't yodel. And he doesn't
repair watches, either. The official laughed and said something
almost admiringly: "'You passed the test".
It was a long time ago since he had such a sense of
achievement. And a very comforting conscience! The driving
license, a small gray card with the photo that had previously
been taken free of charge, made him almost a little proud. And
was urgently needed because without a driver's license
nothing can be achieved in the US.

The following 'scene' cost him more than one Swiss franc. But
had, of course, to be paid in dollars.
One morning in early April, 'his' car was no longer where it
should be. Stolen? He fell into panic. But on the left side of the
street, there were no other cars. The whole street was
completely empty on its left side as far as the eye can see. But
there is no free parking space on the right side.
What's going on here?
The big question mark in his brain must have been noticed by
one of the rare pedestrians. The man now pointed with his
hand at a rusty metal plate set up on an iron post. The words
written on it could only be deciphered with great difficulty.
There was something written like No parking allowed on odd
working days. Snow clearing vehicles in action.

And today it is such a working day!

There was for a long time no white 'stuff' fallen in Minneapolis. Snowfall is rather rare in Minnesota at this time of the year. Fortunately, he remembered from one of his few walks where to find the nearest police station. Nothing more than going there immediately! It was reachable by foot in half an hour. When there is no deep-frozen ice on the sidewalk.

And he has a driver's license!!!

The car was there. Huge relief. The procedure with the police officer and the penalty to be paid were moderate according to the given circumstances.
He willingly 'shoveled' a few dollars over the table.
The official on duty was also very friendly. He almost seemed to have pity with for the little Swiss. He asked mischievously: "Don't you have snow in Switzerland? And do you have snow clearing vehicles?"

Another car story. This time, not a real one. It is a joke. But as it is in every joke, there is always a certain statement behind it. In the joke which now follows, there are IT people involved.
A hardware engineer, a software specialist, and a computer salesman are sitting in a car. They had to drive down a hill on a small, steep road.
The car moves faster and faster. The driver loses control over the vehicle. They are sweating and in a horrible panic.
But, oh wonder, the car suddenly stops. Barely one step away from the edge of the canyon deep below.
They jump out of the car and are totally exhausted.
After a while, the engineer stands up, takes his toolbox, opens the hub, and starts to work while saying; "I will fix this".
The salesman lays back and said calmly: "Forget it. I will sell this car".
The programmer shakes his head and said seriously: "No, no. Why don't we go up again and see if the problem is repeatable?"

4.6. The Architecture of the Supercomputer.

The next stage of the training was now in Arden Hills. This is an Eastern suburb of Minneapolis on the other side of the 'old man river'. An immense flat building with no windows. The interior was very simple. The partitions between the small offices are made of plywood. In the middle was the room for meals. Equipped with vending machines and automates which spat out very hot black stuff. The training room was a bit larger. With stools without a backrest. They were not so necessary because most of the discussions were done standing up. And those were loud, intensive, and very frequent. It was gesticulated wildly with arms and hands. In the same group with him were only Americans from the various US States. From New York, Oklahoma, Texas, and Arizona to California.

There were more than only a few uncertainties about what they were told by the very insecure teacher. So, the telephone to the lab in Chippewa Falls in western Wisconsin was running hot. There, the machine was developed.

But there is no question about its most modern architecture and hardware. The 6600 was three times faster than the previous record-holder, the IBM 7030 Stretch. This alarmed IBM. The at that time CEO, Thomas Watson Jr. wrote a memo to his employees: "Last week, Control Data announced the 6600 system. I understand that in the laboratory developing the system, there are only 34 people, including the janitor. Of these, 14 are engineers and 4 are programmers. Contrasting this modest effort with our vast development activities, I fail to understand why we have lost our industry leadership position by letting someone else offer the world's most powerful computer". Cray's reply was sardonic: "It seems like Mr. Watson has answered his own question".

Another of Seymour's quotes was this: "It is not enough to build the fastest CPU. More important is the performance of the overall system".

The central processor (CPU) consists of the following components:

Eight 60-bit 'X' registers. They contain the operands in the form of integers with 20 octal digits. The first bit determines whether the number is positive or negative. Or with floating-point values in which the first bit also determines whether it is a positive or negative value. The second bit indicates whether the efficient is positive or negative. The efficient is 10 bits, the coefficient is 48 bits long.

Eight 18-bit 'B' registers. They are mostly used for indexes in tables. B0 always had to contain the value 'one'. It is used by all CPU programs because the instruction 'Set register Xx to the value in B1' is much faster than the instruction: 'Set register Xx to 000000000000000000001'

Eight 18-bit 'A' registers. They contain the memory addresses. These are used to address the program instructions and the data needed by the programs.

The size of the central memory is 128 kilobytes

Then there are the 10 actual 'computing' functional units: 2 Adders, 2 Counters, 2 Multipliers, 1 Shift, 1 Boolean, and 1 Branch. For each of these operations, here is dedicated hardware.

Then there are the so-called peripheral processors, the PPUs. These are small computers with a memory of 4096 12-bit words. The instruction set is adapted to control the peripheral devices. The set consists of 64 12-bit orders.

The 'computing' hardware components for all ten PPUs exist only once. It serves all ten small processors. One after the other uses the same hardware. The PPUs 'circulate' in a circle, the so-called 'barrel'. Each of them is assigned 100 nanoseconds of the 'actual' processor time. The 'barrel' turns once in a microsecond. The memories of the PPUs are accessed in the 900 remaining nanoseconds.

There is one very sophisticated instruction in the instruction set of the PPUs is the so-called 'Exchange Jump' (octal code 260x). This triggers the exchange between programs in the central processor. All registers described above plus a reference address for each program, current position within the program ('P' address), and other program-specific information are exchanged in one 'go'. This is the easiest way to accomplish a system to efficiently handle the needs required to achieve the multitasking feature.

4.7. The Hardware of the Supercomputer.

Now to the actual physical description of the 'touchable' hardware.

The memories are magnetic core memories. Tiny magnetic rings contain the values zero or one. Five fine wires are pulled through the wafer-thin rings. Four, two vertically and two horizontally, to address the ring. One diagonally for 'demagnetizing' and reading out the stored bits. As being said: A 'one' or a 'zero'.

The manufacturing of such storage devices was a delicate and extremely precise task. A memory unit of 20x25 centimeters in size and the capacity of 4096 12-bit words used in the 6000 series had the proud price of around eight thousand Swiss Francs. For comparison, a new Volkswagen Beetle had at that time about the same price.

The 6600 memory contents are not checked for errors, as was most common in computers, through a control bit (parity bit). To quote Seymour Cray: "If a parity check is necessary, then the core memory is no good". One of the typical no-so-appreciated side-note from Seymour.

Therefore, a customer, the LRL (Lawrence Radiation Laboratory), requested a special instruction in the central processor. The so-called 'population counter', octal code 43. It counts the bits in the X register. So, later it can be checked whether everything is still there as should be.

The approximately 400000 silicon transistors with the size 5x5x8 millimetexors are tightly packed in the so-called module. A module has the size of 3x10x10 centimeter and contained up to 64 concrete transistors. At the back of the module are gold-plated 5 millimeters long pins. The holes in the frame where the modules are screwed in are also gold-coated. The two wires (twisted pairs cables) that connect the modules to each other are plugged into at the rear.

There are x different variations of modules. Depending on the function to be performed. 20 such modules are mounted on a frame. These frames contain inside a tube. Through these tubes flows cooled liquid Freon to cool the heat generated by the transistors. Twenty of these frames are mounted in the so-called chassis. 4 of these chassis are in turn located in one of the large four cabinets. The chassis can be opened like a big door. Chassis Nr. one contained all the components and memories of the PPUs. Chassis Nr. five contained the hardware needed for the so-called 'Scoreboard'. At the outer ends of the very heavy metal cabinets are the refrigeration-producing equipment, the pumps, and the components for the power supply. The 4 cabinets are arranged in a right-angled cross. To keep the distance between the modules as small as possible. The electric current in a wire takes about one nanosecond to 'travel' 15 centimeters. Everything in the 6600 is extremely and exactly, tightly calculated.

The basic 'logic' used is the same in every computer. And this holds also true for the latest terabit 'clocked' super microprocessors.

- The logical functions 'and', 'or', 'nand', 'nor', 'xor', and 'xnor'
- The semi-stable transistor array, the temporary 1-bit memories.
 - The clock pulses are multiplied and distributed to every module.

Minneapolis is over now. The next time he comes back here is another computer 'story', Then, he will be a 'softy'. That means a software specialist.

41. CDC 6000 Transistor Module   **42. Transistor module**

43. CDC 6000 Memory Unit   **44. CDC Memory Plate**

5. Chippewa Falls and Eau Claire, Wisconsin.

5.1. Hands-on CDC6600 Serial Nr. 3.

The chance to get to know Seymour Cray personally became concrete. Because now he was transferred to Chippewa Falls, Wisconsin. In the factory, or better the laboratory, where the 6600 was built. At the time, the 'monster' was still in development. It will take years until the supercomputer worked more or less error-free. In particular, the software.

The laboratory is located next to Cray's birth house. Idyllically situated on the banks of a picturesque little river. An environment that will soon become, autumn is approaching, more and increasingly colorful.
 Seymour and his crew are about to finish the machine with serial number 3. The one that was ordered by CERN and must be delivered in January next year (1965). The engineer who is, among others, then responsible for it, namely him, can therefore deal with the pitfalls of serial 3 from the very beginning. And there were more than enough of such those.
It was very impressive to see the future trouble-maker in nature. He was almost scared. But he bravely plunges into the adventure. As an experienced pragmatist, he was here much more convenient than with the dry, often confusing, and even very incomplete theoretical schooling.
Many facts were here in Chippewa Falls, very new and entirely different from what he had imagined.
It is best to start with the beginning. How is the whole complexity initiated? How do you start such a supercomputer? This is surprisingly simple and also logically comprehensible. On a door outside one of the cabinets, there is a matrix with 12x12 toggle switches. Corresponding to the twelve bits of a PPU instruction. It allows programming 12 PPU commands. The initial start program is thus entered by the position of the switches. The possible variants of this process are therefore very limited. But it is enough to control a card-reader and read a punched card. The card has punched in binary the next

program, which then reads in the operating system from a magnetic tape. This card, for some reason, was always blue, It contains further instructions in binary format. This requires many holes and makes the card very vulnerable to defects. Therefore, a copy of the card must be available at all times. He soon was able to read the code on the card with his eyes without mechanical or electronic help. In an emergency, it was also possible to make corrections by closing one or more holes with tiny bits of paper or by inserting additional holes with a little hand-activated card-puncher.

The 6600 can only be started when at least the card-reader and one of the connected tape stations is in working condition, By activating the 'dead-start' switch at the bottom of the switch array, the whole 6600 is initialized. This means that all bi-stable elements, the flip-flops, were set to zero and the small start program specified with the mechanical switches is triggered.

When the tape with the operating system has been read, which could take minutes, the machine was ready for 'actions'. First, there are questions required for the further course of starting and configuring the operating system are displayed on the operating console, Now, an operator controls the further actions by using the keyboard.

Such commands could be simple to enter the current date and time, commands for removing and adding peripheral devices, and so on. Later, when the OS was running then orders like stopping a program, changing the priority of a program, assigning tape units to a user program and so on, are given via this console. This console is also the most modern of the modern. Until now, the control units were long, flat boxes like large tables. Equipped with push buttons or mechanical switches and little lamps. LEDs (Light-Emitting Diodes) were at that time far from being available.

The numbers and letters appear on the front of the two cathode-ray tubes. They are 'chased' there by a voltage of 15,000 volts. This device is always admired by everybody and not only by him. From further away, the display tubes look like the huge eyes of prehistoric frogs. Does the name 6600 come from these? The two zeros could have been derived from the two eyes of an animal.

Seymour Cray has subordinated himself to the Marketing Manager and no longer named the 6600 after the street building number or his laboratory, like the 1604 or others. Only Seymour knows the reason.

After a week of becoming familiar with the start procedure, he was thrown into the hot pot of hard work. His job was now to help to plug the wires between the modules in a frame. The first useful action was the adjustment of the wire length between the modules. Why 'tune' the wire length? Can't one just use the shortest possible wire?

Not at all! Because there are short-term registers with a length of 120 bits. For example, for buffering double-precision floating-point numbers. Twenty modules were needed for this. They all are timed by the clock pulse. That's why the length of the wire between the clock pulse distributor and the modules must be the same. This thickened the 'mattress' of the wires behind the chassis enormously. The control was carried out by observing the incoming pulses using a cathode ray oscilloscope, which simultaneously records four different signals. A very expensive device. Therefore, there was only one of those available in the laboratory.

It was not the only reason why work had to be carried out around the clock. In four shifts. The machine must be finished as quickly as possible. In addition, it is also used for the development of the software, teaching operators, and the training of the maintenance personnel.

45. Dead Start Panel

46. Temperatures Control Panel

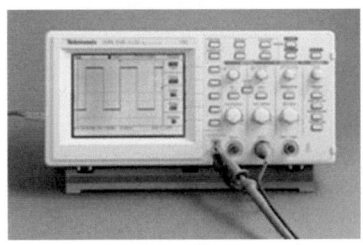

47. Cathode Ray Oscilloscope

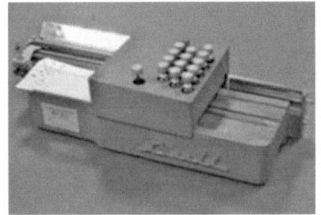

48. Hand Card Puncher

5.2. Critical problems, challenges, and 'Mysteries'.

But back to work. There is still a lot more to do than just a few things.
A big problem occurred. Misunderstandings came up for everyone, Including Seymour. The perfidious difficulty was only found after weeks.
The switching time of the chosen transistors must, according to the specifications, be between four and five nanoseconds.

Now, there were two different deliveries of those. The first had a switching time of just below the upper tolerance limit. The second delivery had a switching time just above the lower guideline. But all within the specified time. So, where was the problem? In retrospect, simple: If 20 transistors with the longer switching time were connected in series, then the total time for a signal to pass was 18 nanoseconds longer, than the time when 20 transistors with the faster switching time were connected in series. This results in a discrepancy, which was deadly for the proper functionality of certain instructions dealing with double-precision numbers.
In order to master this fatal fact, the following means were used: The speed of the electrical impulses was artificially delayed by about 0.5 nanoseconds. This was accomplished by screwing a funny little cap made of silver onto the test points of the modules that were involved in the problem. If the test program now runs ok, then the famous error caused by the different switching times was found.

A very critical machine part is the so-called 'scoreboard'. It is needed for the proper parallel processing of the arithmetic operations. The control of the availability of the receiving X register is very demanding and almost impossible. A sophisticated test program designed for this purpose was created: The CT3 (Central Processor Test No. 3). A random number generator generates a sequence of arithmetic operation instructions. At first, they are carried out as normal in the hardware made for them. Then the same operations are repeated by other functional units and/or in the PPUs, so to speak simulated. Then the results are compared. If they match, everything is fine. If not, then the devil of troubleshooting starts.
Nothing for him yet. Only very knowledgeable engineers are able to solve such a problem. The CT3 will continue to be used for years. The number of rounds, i.e. the sequences of the operation that are always different, is noted exactly and then transmitted to the other locations which use a 6600. The installations all over the world compete which each other. Which one of the delivered 6600 brought the most error-free cycles over the stage? Initially, the intervals between error-free

sequences were freighting short!

A 'mystery' is the generation of the clock pulse. The 6600 has none of the commonly used crystals that vibrate at an absolutely precise frequency. By connecting some transistors to each other by wires of different lengths, a clock time of 100 nanoseconds is generated. Nobody was able to explain to him exactly how this works in detail. And this was puzzling most of the other specialists too.
This clock frequency was by far faster than those of any other computer in the world at that time.

5.3. 'Stories' from Chippewa Falls.

The mood, the team spirit, and the mutual respect of all employees engaged in the lab, almost only the male gender, was excellent. Very, very rarely a loud word or even a heated discussion. Only once did he see Seymour angry. A marketing manager from the headquarters wanted him to create a compiler for the programming language COBOL (Common Business-Oriented Language). The architecture of the 6600 is completely unsuitable for this. It was created to be the world's fastest scientific machine. The 'marketing freak' was then promptly thrown out of the lab by Seymour.

But once, the genius was also very satisfied. Another of his creations was sold. For roughly 2 million dollars. He ordered to buy all real French champagne to be found in Chippewa Falls. There were only three bottles available!

To his excitement, the 'father of Supercomputers' took his time to chat with a Swiss 'learner', namely him. In the front of the Lab in the most beautiful sunny fall weather. They sat quietly together in front of the building, drinking a cup of coffee together.

Once Seymour organized a meeting of the foreign trainees with the members of the local Rotary Club where he was an active member. There were three from Europe: A colleague from Germany, he, and a specialist for cooling devices from Geneva. This man was absolutely needed for the maintenance of the 6600.

They were invited to dinner in the only hotel in town and afterward interviewed by the editor of the local newspaper. They appeared in the paper the next day on the front page. With a group photo entitled: "CDC trains engineers from Europe in Chippewa Falls".

He could already express himself quite well in American English. This was registered with something like admiration by the villagers. He was soon very popular in the only bar in the village. The other guests were very curious and wanted to know a lot about him and Switzerland. And offered him a glass of beer, only to hear him speak. His foreign accent in the pronunciation was here extremely rare.

On the wall in the bar hung two handwritten posters. They were written with a red colored pencil:

We have an agreement with the bank. The bank does not sell beer, and we do not give credits.
In God, we trust. All others pay cash.

In the same shabby building was a restaurant called 'steak house'. There, soon will be served the usual Christmas dinner at a very reasonable price, namely 3 dollars. Lobster and steaks as much as you want. The price was very cheap for him, even though the dollar was at the time 4.30 CHF.
 In general, the prices were at that time in Minnesota very low. A hamburger at the tiny, small plywood stand of the chain 'White Castle' in downtown Minneapolis costs just 10 cents! A gallon of fuel was available for 18 cents thanks to the price war of the petrol stations. If he filled his car up twice in a row, then the washing of the car was for free. The just-released racy and very charming Ford Mustang had a modest price of 2450 dollars.

The jar of beer at 'Leinis' was with 25 cents, almost

overpriced. This is or was a kind of garden restaurant, a little outside the town. The name comes from its owner. An immigrant from Bavaria named Leinenkugel. The man also brought his beer brewing art with him and brewed the Leinenkugel beer. A local specialty brewed according to the German purity law. As Mr. Leinenkugel emphasized over and over again.

Alcohol was not allowed in the United States outdoors or in public gardens. Was (or is it still?) state or federal law? This was very unfortunate! Because the restaurant was beautifully situated on one of the many lakes. It was the meeting point for young people like him. There were also some from the neighboring state. Because in Wisconsin, unlike Minnesota, beer consumption was allowed from the age of 18 on. The pubs near the state border were truly thankful.

49. Chippewa Falls, Wisconsin   **50. Leinenkugels Brewery**

5.4. The end of a great year.

He lived with his German colleague in Eau Claire. This is a bigger place, about 20 km. southwest of Chippewa Falls. At the highway between Minneapolis/St. Paul and Chicago. Where he had to go there soon. To visit the Swiss Consulate in the 'Windy City'. The reason was that he was not able to render his yearly military service. So, he went to Chicago. He wanted anyway to see one day the city where Al Capone organized the mafia crimes.

He found the skyscraper. It had the Swiss cross clearly visible, marked at the entrance. Upstairs, a lady was present in an elegant office. As is a 'must' to properly indicate that Switzerland is a wealthy country. She was in a folk costume, was knitting, and greeted him in the broadest Bernese dialect: "Gruess äch. Was weiter?". In English: "Hi, What do you want?" Then she asked him about his place of residence and address. Then she became extremely furious. Because he said truthfully: "Post Camp 1256, Eau Claire, Wisconsin". She rumbled: "A Swiss doesn't live like you in a warehouse. Are you a gypsy?" But he did not have his own letterbox!

Then he told her that he is (almost, unfortunately) not forever there. And that next year he will do his military duties again as a brave soldier.

In Eau Claire, he lived in a cheap, slightly brittle, older one-story wooden house. With an always grumpy and always ugly female owner. At least the 'hermitage' was always very well heated, or better overheated. This was not bad either. Because from the beginning of December it could get bitterly cold here. It got so icy that his colleague unscrewed the battery of his old Volkswagen in the evening to keep it warm under the bed during the night.

One day, the mayor of the city invited him for dinner, The reason was that, despite its French name, no other foreigners were living there.

Now, it is time to return to Switzerland. He had a whole full year of joy, excitement, efforts, and experiences behind him:

He learned English!
He learned to drive a car!
He learned a lot about the Supercomputer!
He met Seymour Cray!

Almost something like being a little sad, he said 'Farewell' to the places which enabled him the great start of his professional career.

- **51. Eau Claire, Wisconsin**

6. The CDC 6600 at CERN. (1965-1972)

6.1. The work with the CDC Supercomputer at CERN.

His American colleagues were fighting for getting an assignment to work at CERN. It was definitely more attractive than the LRL or at New York University. Or at an installation in a secret military base somewhere between the Mississippi and the Rocky Mountains.

Shortly after the machine was delivered, the long-lasting time of his work at CERN began. The machine was installed by specialists from Chippewa Falls. He was just a spectator and was used as a henchman. For example, to get coffee for the others. Some of his American teammates spit it promptly out. For them, it tasted so unusually different and strong. They were not at all used to this.

The electrical power supply machines needed by the computer were entirely new to him and incredibly impressive. The CDC 6000 Series computers are powered with 60 and 400 Hertz AC. The voltage, which is common in Europe, has the frequency of 50 Hertz and must therefore be converted.

Why 400 Hertz? Quite simply because the conversion to direct current is easier to achieve. The conversion to DC is performed in the 6000 series machines themselves.

Four huge converters are installed in a kind of machine hall which was specially built for this purpose. Why two each? Not because of their performance. But because of the highly unlikely case of a failure of one of the converters. In the computer world, at least one or more technical resources as the reserve are a must. The whole room looks like the generator hall of a small hydropower plant. Huge electric motors are mechanically coupled with equally huge generators. Those machines create a loud noise of around 90 decibels. It is so big that it could still be heard in summer through the then open doors in the nearby 'Village' Meyrin, 5 kilometers away. And accordingly also provoked the expected complaints by the people living there!

Most of the maintenance engineers lived there too. This was a good thing. Because in the case of the frightening and unfortunately too frequent breakdowns of the system, the man on duty can immediately request help from others. The team functioned extremely well. It could happen that everyone was at the same time at the same party. One phone call was enough and the entire CDC staffs in Geneva, including managers, salesmen, and software specialists were in the computer room at nearly 'lightning speed'.

Not only in the event of a breakdown were 'all men on deck'. Even with such tedious work. A tremendous exercise soon came up to them. All wires between the chassis in one cabinet to the other had to be replaced in a 'night and fog' action (German expression for something which has to be done at nights and should not be seen by anybody) This was done over a weekend. About 2000 cables had to be replaced. The reason for this was found out very late. The small adapter plugs required for the connections between the cabinets had not been tinned carefully enough. As a result, the material corroded and fractions of a nanosecond of the impulses flowing through the wires got lost. They had to be replaced by connectors coated with a nanometer-thick cover of gold. Only two connections of 2000 were incorrectly wired. A masterpiece by all those involved.

There were many others and at first not comprehensible errors in the hardware. And also in the software! Much to the displeasure of the customer. The scientists at CERN were, again in his own humble opinion, very tolerant, understandable, and friendly with the CDC personnel.

There was a little fidgety and always nervous Dutchman. A genius in what numbers are concerned. Among other things, the man was able to quote the SBB's (Swiss federal trains) timetable by heart. He told him once: "The 6600 is great. When it works!"

And then there was the computer 'which'. A small, not-so-good-looking Englishwoman. A very, very talented and brilliant programmer. She could get outraged, and then she shouted so loud that the screams even exceeded the noise of the generators. And then, like a witch, she rushed away. Without a broom, but with a huge stack of paper under her arm and cursing loudly.

And then there was the typical Scottish gentleman, a Mac ... A doctor of mathematics and the head of computer science at CERN at that time. He was not at all angry about the current unreliability of his risky acquisition. He must have known that a Supercomputer like the 6600 has its 'birth pains'.

After all, the 6600 at CERN set the at that time the world record for calculating the famous number 'Pi' with 50 thousand digits after the comma.

The reliability of the 6600 had urgently to be improved. He and his colleagues were challenged to the utmost. The breakdowns must also be repaired more quickly. They had a few 'tricks' in their closet. For example, using a hairdryer. Suspicious rows of modules, which could be a source of the problem, are warmed up while test programs are running. In the hope to find the weak points earlier.

Another, probably in retrospect, the completely nonsensical procedure was this: To leave the heavy chassis with the 400 modules open at an angle of exactly 30 degrees for better cooling.

There was a special real story worth mentioning. Because it occurred in his career only once: Total fallout of one of the two large display tubes of the control console!

This was not the case for him. Because he was not a radio nor TV electrician. And unfortunately, he could not learn FEAM. What is now completely forgotten and is not of any importance anymore.

The very high tensions needed for the console tubes terrified him also terribly. Fortunately, he had a good colleague, a certified electric engineer. The man first had great fun provingt his capability to fix, them for the momentary only 'one-eyed' console.

Not for a long time!

The specialist soon found out that a condenser in there has burned out. The problem was therefore clearly recognized immediately and can therefore be solved in a relatively short time. But this time it was not repaired as fast as desired. Because in the local CDC spare parts warehouse, there were no such components. And this part could not be found throughout the entire CERN.

Quote: "Necessity is the mother of invention".

His colleague reacted very fast. He raced home in his old VW Beetle. There he took his TV apart. He found there the so much-needed capacitor with exactly the right capacity!

The situation was saved once more ...

A repetitive problem was caused by the units which contain the RAM core memories. These components cannot be repaired locally and must be flown to the manufacturer in the USA. At the moment, the producing company is totally overwhelmed with work.

The engineers at CERN soon had the suspicion that the modules they send to be repaired were sent back without ever being touched by the manufacturer! They had to find a way to see that their supposition was right. They marked the outgoing defect units with a tiny hand-marked 'C', standing for CERN, under the top metal cover plate. All new incoming allegedly repaired units were checked immediately. If such a 'C' was there, then they were placed at the end of the local queue of spare units or even sent back right away without even first trying to use it.

But there was also more enjoyable news to report from CERN.

For example: Eating in the 'workers' canteen on the very edge of the site. The owner and at the same time also the cook was French. His 'Coq au vin', which is chicken in wine, was particularly popular with the Americans. Not only because of its volume. The taste of the 'bird' was more than a little different from the 'Kentucky Fried Chicken'.

•

52. CERN, Main Entrance

6.2 The 'hunger' for more and better storage devices.

The need to process huge volumes of more or less usable data was increasing from one day to the next.
The first new device to increase the capacity of very quickly accessible data installed at CERN was the drum storage unit. This accomplished a quick transfer of data streams into the core memory of the CPU.
This imposing 'box', three meters high and two meters long and wide, contained a metal drum of one meter in diameter. The outside of the drum has a magnetic coating. The data were written, read, and erased by an immense number of write/read heads which were fixed at the chassis outside the rotating drum. The drum spins at hundreds of revolutions per

second. The storage capacity of this device is rather modest. But it is very suitable for applications where, as prior, the quick exchange of data is most important.

Another new type of disk storage starts its triumphal success. This time they are smaller devices, 120 centimeters high and 1 meter wide and long. From a distance, they look like an oversized kitchen stool. But don't sit on it! Because at the top is a heavy glass lid with at its top a thick wooden knob of ten centimeters in diameter. If you turn the knob violently and pull the whole 'thing' up, you have the interchangeable disk package in your hand. These are brown magnesium plates that are mounted at a distance of 10 millimeters apart. The great advantage of this 'apparatus' is clear: Only the data which had currently to be 'online' must be present. That means that only the data required by the program currently running in the CPU must physically be present.
Every programmer and every user had their own disk packs. For example, every system programmer has hers/his own version of the operating system. Every user saves their own personal programs and data with the portable disc pack.
The plate packs already had quite a large capacity. The first model had a volume of 40 Megabytes. Then, followed the models, which hold up to 300 Megabytes of data. At first, they had, for computer components atypically, a fair price.
CERN had many of them. The weight of such a disc pack should also be mentioned. It was just a few ounces less than the maximum weight that was allowed to be carried at a workplace by female employees under American law.

Another unique 'creation' was the ECS (Extended Core Storage). This was an additional standalone core storage device. Again in its own large closet with the size of the mainframe. Equipped with large frames, 80x120 centimeters, which contained very tiny magnetic rings. The capacity was rather modest. But the access time is very rapid. And the ECS was again very susceptible to failure.
That is why the weak and very feeble soccer team which was made up of operating personnel and system programmers at CERN was called 'ECS'. The team participated in the CERN

internal soccer championship. He played with them. And also scored a sensational goal. With the head! On a corner kicked by an Austrian! International cooperation in perfection!

53. Drum Storage Device   **54. Disk Pack Drive**

55. Portable Disc Pack Drives

●

6.3. The Baseball Game.

CERN had a very expensive maintenance contract that required that a technician had to be present 24 hours. The contract also covered holidays, like Christmas and New Year's Day. No problem for him. He was not necessarily a friend of festive days. Especially in the hours without problems, on

92

weekends and during holidays, something at that time was very new and also very popular. And it killed the sitting around and waiting to be useful.

What was this? The Baseball Game at the operation control console.

It was most likely the first game ever programmed for a 'von Neumann' machine.

Indeed, very cleverly programmed by someone who unfortunately remained unknown to him.

A little stick figure appears at the bottom of one of the console's display tubes. Above was another. The most important man in real baseball: The pitcher. At the push of a key, the 'virtual' pitcher throws the baseball down towards the 'virtual' batter. Sometimes fast, sometimes slowly, sometimes straight, sometimes in a curve. Just like in American baseball. The batter at the bottom of the console must now react. The player at the console had to press one of the two programmed keys on the keyboard. Depending on the speed of his reaction and the intensity of the keystroke, the 'baseball', a small dot on the screen, fly away or sneaks slowly along the bottom line. In the best case, this results in a 'home run'. The best which can result in real baseball. If not then, depending on the reaction of the batter, there are points given or nothing at all. The results are displayed on one of the screens. There was an ambitious competition between the computer people at CERN to who will achieve the best result. They were coming from different European countries.

He soon lost interest in the game. He rather wanted to program such games himself. What he later did. On a personal computer of the first PC generation: The Commodore Vic-20.

6.4. His toughest problem and his biggest flop.

After three years, he was promoted to EIC (Engineer in Charge). This meant a lot of additional responsibility and additional worries for him. One problem, in particular, brought him sleepless nights to the brink of despair. The machine 'crashed' very often. That means the screens of the operating console were suddenly white. The blank screen effect! Or other phenomena, which were catastrophic to the overall functioning of the system, occurred.

In such a case was the analysis of the contents of the core memory needed. This is the registration of all data in the memory, and of the bi-stable storage elements on a magnetic tape before the machine was restarted. This is called the "post-mortem memory dump". The whole immense amount of data is then printed on a line printer in octal numbers on a huge list of 100 characters per line and 100 lines per page. These are now analyzed by the maintenance personnel and the system programmers to track down the error.

He soon had bundles of such paper on his desk. They were laboriously 'plowed' through. At first, without being able to draw any conclusions. But one day the enlightenment came. In the part of the small memory of the PPUs where the permanent program parts were stored were individual bits missing.

Easy to repair: Replace the core memories.
Did not help!
Replace the modules that receive the data from the memories.
Did not help!
Replace all the modules responsible for the PPUs one after the other. So. all 400 in chassis number one.
Did not help!
Replace all power supply elements in chassis one.
Did not help!
Once again, he felt like the biggest donkey on the mountain.

But now came the proof of the quote from Maria von Ebner-Eschenbach: "Coincidence is a necessity shrouded in veils". One night, shortly after midnight, he sat bored, tired, and humiliated in front of the console.
Like hundreds of hours before. The maintenance program

that tests the memory of the PPUs was running. So far, there was no sight of the slightest trace of an error. Restless and already falling into fatal thoughtlessness, he slowly rolled back and forth, monotonously sitting on the comfortable armchair equipped with wheels in front of the console.

And then it happened!!!

A huge spark hissed between the arm of the chair and the aluminum table of the console.
And the test program whistles!
A big problem!
A 'fatal error'!

And it was the same type of failure that had been desperately searched for several months: Bits were missing in the permanent part of the memory in a PPU.
Now, immediately try to provoke the same failure again. To his wonderful relief, the same problem appeared again.
The greatest salvation!
Because with computers, their programs, and in computer science in general, a problem is solvable as soon as it can be reproduced.
Then it's 'only' a matter of time before it is solved. How long this time then really is, is another question.

The cause of the lost bits was briefly explained. It was the static electricity in the room. Later measurements by a specialist from CERN showed values up to a voltage of 1000 volts!

As a first treatment, a fence, made of hemp ropes, was drawn around the entire computer.
Visitors were no longer allowed in the computer room. The very few female programmers were instructed to wear only cotton skirts and no silky underwear.

As a further measure, a specialist from Minneapolis was flown in. The problem had been avoided if all components in the machine had been correctly connected to the earth. The engineer came. First of all, he wanted to see the reproduction of the problem himself.

He saw it!

Then he said: "I have to try that in the laboratory". But there they had only wooden stools without wheels at the console.

The 'guy' was, in fact, very sympathetic. The man was for the first time outside the USA, and therefore was more than just slightly insecure.
They went together to eat cheese fondue. At a famous restaurant for Swiss specialties in the city center.
It tasted excellent for the man from Minneapolis. Due to a lack of language skills and self-confidence, the jovial gentleman was every day of his stay in Geneva only eating cheese Fondue...

After the success of having explained the catastrophic behavior of the machine came a disaster. It arrived during the wholly failed outplacement for three months to the Technical University of Aachen in Germany. He was 'ordered' there to train and to help the very freshly engaged local technicians.
This brought him his biggest flop in his 'career' as a hardware engineer.
A big problem, a failure of a group of write/read heads in the CDC 6603 disk storage unit. Sure that this was a problem for him. And what a big one! He could not solve it. Why: Lacking detailed knowledge of the device? He must have slept in Minneapolis that day when the CDC 6603 was in the training program. Or was he in love with Alice?
The customer foamed with rage. His boss as well. To fly in a specialist from Minneapolis would take too much time. Time with the computer was extremely precious because the many students were really greedy to use it.

Immediate action was urgently needed. A software specialist from CERN was flown to Düsseldorf. In the next available free seat in an airplane. And driving on the highway to Aachen at the highest possible speed. The man's task was to make changes in the OS software so that the defective heads were no longer addressed. The allocation of the places on the disk and thus the control of the write/read heads was done by a table in the operating system, the so-called 'TRT' (Track Reservation Table) which contains one bit for each 'track'. If it is a zero, then the track is available. The programmer from CERN had now manually set in the OS all tracks which were addressed by the defective heads to 'reserved'. A mammoth task.

His friend from Geneva did a very good job. The system was soon again operating OK. And the specialist from the USA could take his time. And dear Sir: Help me! Please take your time to explain to the completely incapable maintenance engineer from Switzerland what he had done wrong to solve that 'dammed' problem.

56. CDC 6600 Operator Console

7. Software (1972-1978).

7.1. His beginning in the software.

During one of the three weeks repetition course in the Swiss Air Force, a simple soldier like him started a discussion about computers. The comrade was never in contact with IT. He asked the following: "What is software?"
 He, the IT Specialist, replied: "Software is something which never works as it should, nobody really understands and which costs a lot. And it is also like tropical fruits. It ripens after being delivered to the customer".
Seymour Cray was also once a programmer.
And here is another quote from him: "I don't do anything in hardware what can be done with software". This quote is again atypical for species like the 'softies'. One of the many of Seymour's typically controversial statements.
The job as EIC was super and became easier every day. Computers were also, since his beginning with CDC, by now something like his hobby.
There were now increasingly longer intervals between urgent, extremely unwanted, stressful, and demanding 'fire fighting' exercises. This was leaving him more time to play baseball with the machine.
But soon the job of a maintenance engineer was not only because of the increasingly monotonous daily duties getting boring. The shift work, especially those that start at midnight, was slowly but surely plaguing. And he, like everybody, got older.
That the maintenance of hardware, not only for the more than embarrassing incident in Aachen, became soon very unpleasant to him must his boss, an uncharacteristically straightforward human and not only money-oriented American, have noticed.

He suggests to he to become the chief of a maintenance team. In computer jargon: To get 'kicked upward'. With, of course, a corresponding increase in wages. This method of promotion was often used to get rid of technical 'nuts'. Or of otherwise for the required job incapable personnel.

He refused.

Why? He preferred to fight lost bits, too slow transistors, shaky wires, and tagged components than to sign expense bills, coordinate missions, and vacation plans, and i from the bad moods of his subordinates.

But now, something new had to come. He had heard 'through the flower' (This is an expression in German when one hears unofficial information) that an American programmer colleague, a member of the CDC crew at CERN, was fed up with the nearly daily embarrassing crashes of the OS. Or had the man simply enough of 'Raclette' and 'Fondue'?

He does not know what the colleague's real reason was. And it doesn't matter. The important thing is that there was a vacancy in the software group. Their boss, a very correct and calm British gentleman, was also a good personal friend.

So, why not start to 'push'?Said and done! He got the job! Although not yet as a senior analyst. This was also, as always should be into the computer world, logical. Does he have to start at the bottom again?

Yes: As a junior programmer.

But he already knew what this new 'profession' could bring. And knew what will wait for him. But the obligatory shift work is over. Although very often he will have to work at night and on weekends and festivities days. Because during the working days, the machine is only available to the customer. So, to speak in 'production'. To test the improvements or, more correctly, the corrections of the many unpleasantly often occurring software 'bugs' was not possible, even at CERN, during the normal working hours.

Nevertheless, It was a great and excellent opportunity to change something one's more in life!

He does not have to start from scratch. He knows the machine language of the 6000 series computer by heart. He learned it with the toggle switches of the dead start panel and by reading and analyzing the hundreds of thousand octal numbers in a postmortem dump.

All eleven processors, the 10 of the PPU and the CPU, have the ability to write and to read any address in the main memory. The absolute taboo for all programs is to write into central memory address zero. This address must always be without any bit. It is used by all programs to clear the contents of the registers.

But masses of programs contain masses of errors. It happened again and again that the memory address zero was overwritten. This resulted in a system crash, a so-called 'bad monitor request'.

This requires, of course, a memory dump to find the cause of the disaster. Again, reading long lists of octal numbers. Pondering for hours was needed to find the 'culprit'. Daylong study of the source code written in ASSEMBLER If several times the roughly same constellation of programs is present in the dump, then the 'sinner' will soon be found. Soon? That's relative. It can take weeks!
Common quotes from every computer specialist: "We will have it solved soon". And then it takes weeks... Or: "The problem is very complicated". And then it's done in an hour...

The CDC customers had, what was not common in the industry, insight access to the source code of the OS.
This was for IBM clients completely out of 'sight'.
And the CDC customers liked this well to add their own wishes. This means they were able to make their own changes to the OS. That makes the installation of a new version of the OS extremely difficult. The local additions and changes must be transferred into the new release. To test everything correctly takes months and night shift work nearly endlessly. Such version changes are also quite common. And when the new version with the CERN-specific changes finally was ready for production, then came the critical first day of probation. Where the adrenalin level of all programmers involved was at its peak.

A popular part of the specific customer requirements for the OS is the 'Scheduler'. That is the program that assigns the individual user program central processor time. Which user or program has the highest priority? Endless controversy and endless suggestions for changes are not inevitable.

Other customer-specific adaptations were allowed theoretically and were also made. Such an addition to the standard OS then made him very worried and required extreme large activation of the brain cells. Because it contained an error that 'killed' the OS.

He found it!

A programmer from CERN, a peaceful Italian, had created the 'faux pas'. He wrote a driver for a printer which was not supported by CDC. The controlling and the sending of data to a peripheral device were accomplished via one of the twelve hardware channels. A peripheral device is physically connected to such a channel. The driver programs in a PPU use it for in- or output of data. More than one PPU program could want to use the same channel at the same time. So, the program must first check if the channel is in use. If not, it can reserve it and therefore lock other programs out. There is an instruction that asks for the availability of the channel. If yes, another Instruction reserves the channel. The instruction which reserves the channel must immediately follow the one which asks for availability. Now, the program created by the local programmer and which caused the crash of the OS did not do it as should be done. After the questionfabout the availability of the channel and its reservation, only a few others followed. Enough to allow another PPU program to get hold of the channel. Two programs were using the same channel at the same time. Deadly to the OS.

The friendly Italian paid, as it was usual in such cases, for the software crew at CERN a barrel of beer.

Quote: "He, who makes something, makes mistakes".
His own quote: "Doing nothing can also be a mistake. Only: It is more difficult to be proofed".

7.2. Tel Aviv, Israel.

A 'classic' theoretical training is now due again. This time in the capital of Israel. Properly read: In Tel Aviv.
And why in Israel? The Israelis bought a CDC with powerful American financial support. And, as always, the Israelis do not want to depend on others. That is why the maintenance and the further development of the entire system were done by themselves. A basic training session was therefore carried out there. And a foreigner, like him, was exceptionally accepted to participate. Of course, only for a fee. To be paid cash.
Already on the approach to Tel Aviv airport, he got to feel the 'wind' which is apparently blowing there. He was questioned on the plane by a very inconspicuous little guy for over half an hour. From birth to the present day. And then, with a grinding of teeth, he got permission to leave the airplane.

The school building was extremely well protected. Soldiers were present all over the place. The meager lecture room was equipped with very narrow tables, uncomfortable wooden stools and was in nearly complete darkness.
There was very strict discipline in the classroom. Every day at eight, the door was closed and locked. There were almost none of the by the 'Amis' so popular coffee breaks. The lunch, rather lousy tasting stuff, was brought to the schoolroom by a catering service on a plastic plate. Then they 'struggled' through until 1730h.
The whole situation remained strongly at the basic military training he had gone through. He was also several years older than the Israelis, which were commanded to participate. Most of them were absolute 'computer obsessed' and even more motivated than he.

Nevertheless, he allowed himself each afternoon to take a smoke break. For this purpose, the always closed entrance door was opened specially for him. He walked around in the open, fresh air, almost gasping for breath. Unfortunately, with his travel bag under his arm. It contained the passport, credit cards, and cash. Sure is sure!
This was immediately proved very drastically. Because he put

his bag on the concrete floor before the building. And then he made a few steps away from it. Because in the same building, there was a nice store with elegant silken lady's dresses and lingerie. Exactly what he likes so much!

Suddenly, he was immediately grabbed violently from behind at the arm. And was shouted at by a muscle monster in a bulletproof vest and with a submachine gun targeted at him. In very broken English: "Get your bag!!!".

7.3. Sunnyvale, California.

He survived these three weeks in Tel Aviv.

He got soon the chance to create those famous software errors (bugs) himself. Because he was sent to Sunnyvale in California. Officially, to be trained. But, in fact, he was 'forced' to participate in the development of the existing operating system. This particular operating system has also an exciting story behind it. It was developed very rudimentary by Seymour Cray and a few other geniuses, originally in Chippewa Falls. In order to test the hardware. It was called the Chippewa Operating System (COS.) which should be replaced as soon as possible by something far superior. It never happened! Because the promised 'miracle' under the name SIPROS (Simultaneous Processing Operating System) resulted in one of the bigger flops in the history of the CDC.

Why? Developed by a consortium!!!

The CDC software was for the most part 'caused' in the 'Silicon Valley' between San Francisco and San Jose. In weather, far more humane and more moderate climate than the one in Minnesota.

He needed a while to moderate his typical 'Teutonic' stubbornness, to stop his profile neurosis, and to adapt to the mentality of the Californians.

His usual demands for a certain office comfort had to be profoundly reduced. Because his office was located in a more or less temporary constructed building. But it was prepared for earthquakes. It was situated a little outside the village. In a not very overbuilt area. Surrounded by wide fields planted with tomatoes and the like.

The building was almost identical to the one in Arden Hills. Quadratic, one floor high, with thin wooden walls, provisionally painted in light gray. Windows were only available on the first floor. This was the floor of the 'chiefs'. Depending on at the time position in the hierarchy, they had an office with an outside view. The windows could not be opened. In the four corners of the building were the offices of the best-paid executives.

The rest of the 'workforce' had offices inside the building. In the so-called 'six-packs'. Derived from the until today used packaging of six small Coca-Cola bottles. The six offices were separated by thin walls which formed a unit. They had all the same size, 2x 4 meters. Each was occupied by two 'slaves', the 'normal' programmers. As he was one of them now, too. The telephone calls made or received by the 12 occupants in a six-pack could be heard by everyone. Also, the very personal intimate gossip if it was not whispered. It was also loud in the 'jail'. The offices had to be cooled. The air conditioning of the building was also cheaply built. That's why the noise level was, to say the least, very high.

The card-puncher machines to produce the programs were situated in the corridors and were very much in demand. To get hold of one, he had to reserve it at least one day before. Time on the computer to test the programs was even scarcer. So at three in the morning, there was sometimes a gap (slot) to use the computer alone.

And he had to be alone! Because that his own code will bring the machine into software crash was more common than not. He soon adapted to the given situation and took over the practices of his 'buddies'. For example, to place the required lists, punched cards, and magnetic tapes on an office chair with rolling wheels and then push everything in the computer room. When it was finally free for one hour.

He was here to learn and had to go through this 'apprenticeship'. With very little experience as a programmer, and therefore he was often very helpless. But the guys there and the in California also surprisingly many lady-programmers took care of him.

There was a small, luckily rather also introverted guy, with him in the same 'chamber'. A Latino from Mexico. This man's work was to write a 'Macro'. Macros were something new to him. There are no such commands in the machine language. It is a construction of a series of often recurring computer instructions. The macro is then called with the necessary parameters and can be used accordingly again and again. The macro his colleagues wrote set an entry in a very important table in the OS, the EST (Equipment Status Table). Such an entry contained all for the control of the peripheral device needed information. And there are many of those: Speed, bandwidth, transmission control, and a lot more equipment-specific information. The creation of such a macro was the full-time job of the newly emigrated little Mexican.

The first task of the beginner from Switzerland, namely him, was to enable the use of the expensive disk space by more than just one computer. So only one copy of the data can serve several machines. And, more important, several machines can over this medium 'talk' to each other.

The coordination of the traffic between the connected machines was a colossal challenge. Especially the 'locking' of the access. It must never be possible for the disc accessing processes of the connected computers to get in each other's way.

First, this entirely new feature was the so-called 'Multi-Mainframe' function. Nobody could imagine at that time what was now started: It was the first step in one of the greatest inventions in the IT world:

The Computer Networks!

Not many inventions on earth had a similar impact on humans.

It was a difficult, highly demanding task for him. But very challenging, and therefore not unwanted. He had to change the existing code which controlled the access to the disk. This part of the OS was called the 'Stack Processor'. Every demand to read/write was first stored in a waiting queue. The stack processor now looks at all the outstanding requests. Then it decides which request to issue first. It is the one that required the shortest movement of the arms, which have the read/write heads attached. Because such a positioning took, relative to the speed of the CPU, a very long time. In other words, the stack processor was optimizing the disc access time for the programs and therefore increased the overall performance of the entire system.

This stack processor did, until now, no need to worry that another machine will use the same disc.

Now it has to check that the disc controller is not accessed by another machine. The stack processor hat before issuing a read/write order to check if the disc controller is free.

Every computer in the multi-mainframe combine had a reserved disc space to write messages to the others. As stated before, the computer network was born!

The lousy working environment put only a little strain on him. Only that his colleague was piling up hundreds of Coca-Cola cans in the narrow space bothers him a lot. He did not even complain. After all, he is just temporary here. And finally, Coca-Cola was at that time to get almost for nothing at Woolworth. And you never know if there will soon be a Coca-Cola shortage!

Like the petrol shortage which occurred. Long lines of cars were waiting in front of the gas stations. If those were open at all. A job for students: The 'car sitter'. They take over the annoying and no money-bringing waiting at the petrol stations.

The comfort in the building was anything else than beyond doubt. In the middle was a, of course, windowless lousy equipped common room for the personnel. With the usual also lousy coffee machines. Their failure rates were even higher than those of the hardware of the 6600 in the first year. A humorist, there are still some of them among the programmers, put labels over the control buttons with the words:

Coffee no cups.
Cups, no coffee.
Water.

Very hot black stuff.

On the wall with the messages to the employees was a poster. To inspire the personnel to work better: "Teamwork sells computers". Below was scribbled in handwriting: "Who got the commission?"

From time to time, there were lectures given by the department chiefs. He had to attend those.
In a modest schoolroom again. With a white, not a black, wallboard.
The well 'build' instructor was currently writing a longer formula for the audience on the board. Suddenly, a violent quake shacked the building. The writing utensil of the speaker sled down ten centimeters. He continued calmly to write, mumbling something like "That was a little earthquake"...
This guy had really nerves made of steel.
Not like him, the student from Switzerland. He was trembling like the leaves on a tree in a hurricane. He is not Californian...
Another event made him even more than only nervous: Bomb alert! Everyone had to leave the building. One hundred meters away, in a tomato field, was the place where the orientation of the workforce took place.
But all had to wait for one, namely Pierre, a Frenchman, and ingenious 'designerr, and let the others wait for a long time. He finally came, strolling comfortably and very slowly. He was apparently used to such alarms from Paris, which were at that time caused by the FNL (Front de Liberation Nationale).

7.4. The Chippewa Operating System (COS)

The CDC 6600 was the first Computer to provide parallel processing. That is. that 5 different programs were actively processed at the same time. Before, only one program at the time was executed.
The operating system software met an entirely different and another approach to implement the new development. It was therefore a very demanding and new challenge to the

programmers.

Seymour Cray and his engineers needed software to thoroughly test their hardware. The officially announced OS SCOPE was far from being usable. So, he and the software crew (Greg Mansfield, Dave Cahlander, and a few others) wrote their own.

The user had to provide the COS first with basic information about his program with the so-called control cards. On those, the username, account number, memory requirements, and the maximal number of tape drives needed at the same time had to be stated. They also contain the calls for the needed compiler, orders for the loader which loaded already compiled code, or other commands like copy files or communicating with the operator. The control cards were followed by the cards with the program statements in the ASSEMBLER language COMPASS or FORTRAN. There was first no user data stored permanently on the disk. The user had to manage his data using magnetic tapes.

The most important part of the COS was the PPU and the CPU Monitor. This code controlled the overall operation of the system. The PPU Monitor Programs ran permanently in PPU Nr. 1. The CPU Monitor managed the central memory, the job scheduler, the already explained Stack Processor, and assigning Tape station to a 'Job'. (A job in the COS is a user program). The CPU Monitor program had, of course, the highest priority.

Five user programs, which were at the same time in the central memory, were controlled by using the so-called control points. On the operator console, the information needed by the operator was displayed. From the console, the operator controlled the job with commands. For example, to 'drop' a job, change its priority, and assign a tape station to the control points. Each job had assigned an area in the central memory. The first address of the bloc was the so-called RA (Reference Address). For the program itself, it was its Address 0. There was no separation between the program code and the program data. This was, of course, very dangerous. It could happen, that for an unknown reason, the program 'jumped' into the data area. This resulted in a big disaster.

The user program could also use only a part of the central memory and therefore were forced to have a rather limited size. There was always a 'fight' between the users for memory space. The programs written by the physicist were often bigger than the maximum memory space the COS was able to provide. Therefore, a very clever and also very complicated method was used: The overlay. This method was to use the assigned memory space for only a part of the program. When this code was executed, then it was 'overlayed' by the next part.

7.5. Laramie, Wyoming.

Now, something happened that was not planned or foreseeable. A volunteer was sought to be present at the University of Laramie, Wyoming. For three months. The obligations there were to wait for a system failure and to be ready to intervene in such a case.
He had no idea where Laramie was. None of his Californian 'Easy Raiders' colleagues wanted to go there. He immediately was ready for it. He loves to see what he never has seen before, and he likes unusual tasks.
And what he will experience there was not so common. Even the flight from Denver to Laramie was adventurous. The pilot of the small twin-engine rattle plane, which was still propelled, checked the tickets personally as the passengers boarded.
The landing at the eastern foot of the Rocky Mountains at an altitude of two thousand meters was surprisingly perfect, despite the rather thick fog and visibility of one hundred meters.
Chapeau Mister Pilot!
At the beginning of October, it was already very cold there. But he was prepared for it. An older Chevrolet was ready for him. The car started immediately despite the cold. The vehicle was

technically in perfect working order. This was good news, because of his experience with third-class car rental companies he did not expect this.

A room in a one-star hotel was also reserved. Clean, huge bed, the bedroom overheated, but unfortunately without a 'minibar'.

The next day he started his work on the huge campus of the university. The name university is a little exaggerated. It was a pretty big school with many students. What they studied there remained a secret to him until today.

The computer was fine. The software was up-to-date. The system was not being used very heavily.

Everything OK! The real likelihood of encountering a problem unknown to him was therefore slim.

But there will be one soon. Fortunately, he wasn't responsible for it and couldn't help. There was a power outage in the house. The main fuse in the computer building gave up its ghost. Cause unknown. He didn't really care.

But the caretaker was in big trouble. Because there was no such a fuse in all of Laramie. It had to be flown in from Denver. This gave him two days without worrying about the system. It took three days until the required fuse reached the town,

For him, time for 'Dolce Fare Niente'. There wasn't much to see in the city. Or rather, in a big 'village' that seemed like a place in an old Wild West movie. There were a couple of large flat malls. With guns and ammunition on the shelves. Then three bars that are reminiscent of the cowboy salons in the middle of nowhere. One of them with a clear bullet hole in the mirror behind the bar counter

Then there was this important railway line. Important for coast-to-coast traffic. With endless crawling freight trains pulled by three locomotives. A street closing barrier could easily be closed for half an hour.

Then there was the very tense traffic of huge trucks of all kinds of transport companies with loudly howling diesel engines. On the very important freeway. Because it is also an east-west crossroad that bypasses the city. And the truck drivers very often stayed in the city overnight. Mostly in one of the wild west movies compliant hotels. With the expected availability of getting female 'attention'. To pay for, of course.

In addition to truck drivers, there were rangers, waitresses, railroad workers, teachers, and some allegedly lazy, useless characters in town.
And real cowboys, too. And every Sunday there was a well-attended rodeo. With him as a spectator. What else could be done here?
What he did was to drive 'his' old Chevrolet deeper into the Rockies on a Sunday. On a seemingly endless ascending road. On the mountain, he was almost shocked. At a sign on the side of the road, he could read the following: Altitude above sea level 10235 feet (~3100 m).
That was almost unbelievable, even for a Swiss.

Wyoming will always be remembered positively and deeply.

57. Laramie Wyoming

7.6. The last days as a System Programmer.

So, he had to work almost 24 hours a day.
But he made it! His changes to the COS were accepted!

He 'offered' a kind of goodbye party with a round of beer to his 'buddies'. In one of the in, California typically, very dark restaurant. His colleagues were thankful to him for his sacrifice

111

to go to the 'Rockies'.

It did not stay with one round of 'Budweiser', 'Coors', or others. Many more bottles were consumed. And were paid for. Not from him anymore.

There was a violent discussion in the typical 'computer Chinese' language. A theme accompanied by sneering laughter was the 'Chinese-Girl Compiler'. This was a CDC project performed in San Diego. The task of an exclusively female Asian group was to write a COBOL compiler for the 6000 series. Something that, as we know, Seymour Cray struggled heavily against. The compiler never reached the 'stage'. It did not have to. The whole 'exercise' had the following reason: The American state department demanded that companies that done business with the state have to employ a certain proportion of emigrants.

Another theme of the 'babbling' was the appreciation of the existing computer languages. One of his colleagues said: "FORTRAN is for students, COBOL is for girls. The only language for men is ASSEMBLER!!!"

This was it for Sunnyvale and his time as an operating system programmer. It was again a very great experience!

58. Sunnyvale, California

7.7. Berlin, Germany.

With FORTRAN, he will soon be ingloriously involved.
Back at CERN began a whole other chapter in the history of
IT. The development in the direction to make it possible for a
user to have direct access to the big mainframes had started.
The application programmer can 'speak' directly with the
machine. The programmer does not need to punch his very
long FORTRAN programs on cards and have them read in by
an operator. And then to have to join the long queue of those
waiting for the results.
He can now type in his program himself into the main memory.
A huge step forward in the still early, but very important, phase
in the history of computer science!
He was very amazed when he could use it for the first time.
Until now, such a possibility was only a highly desirable
'Utopia'.

The mechanical input devices, simply telex machines, were
soon replaced by the so-called monitors. Those were, today
one would say, primitive, TV sets. Of course, still without
Microprocessor or other 'intelligent' electronics. A monochrome
TV with a keyboard. Nothing more and nothing less.
Back to FORTRAN. In the COS, the program to control the
interactive use of the computer was the so-called 'Editor'. It
was written in FORTRAN. This program was a product
produced by one of his close friends. He knew the man from
his time in Sunnyvale.

This editor was probably one of the first in the category of re-
entrant programs. This means, that a single system program
can at the same time simultaneously process the programs of
several users.

Software is known, as previously often mentioned, as a
product like tropical fruits. It rips at the customer side.
The 'Editor' was also far from being 'rip' when the first
provisional version was delivered to CERN. But this new

possibility for everyone to become, as he puts it in German:
'Mit dem Computer per 'DU', was sensational!
Also, for the TH Berlin. A very well-known technical university.
They bought a CDC machine. With very kind support from the
German government in Bonn and the Berlin Senate.

It was long before the fall of the wall.

The clever leaders of the university immediately recognized
the potential of the upcoming trend of interactive computing.
His friend and creator of the multi-user editor were ordered to
Berlin. He was sent there in order to become familiar with the
program.

The flight over the air bridge from Frankfort to East Berlin with
TWA in the very tight rows of seats and fully occupied older
plane was adventurous.
Very dangerous was for him the approach to the Tempelhof
airport in the center of Berlin. Because the assigned corridor
for the landing was very narrow. To the left and right of the
runway, there were huge blocks with flats. It was a bit like
flying through a canyon.
Only slightly milder than landing in Laramie was then the
landing in Berlin.
The editor program had one crash landing after the other. Fell
on its own nose. His friend and creator could experience and
correct his 'bugs' on the spot.
The schooling took place in a large lecture room. With more
than a dozen monitors. And very interested and greedy
students. And a multi-user program that did not survive 15
minutes. The famous mean time between failures was at a
record-breaking minimum.
It was clear that he did not give to the Berliner the fact that he
also works for CDC. Why? He was ashamed of what his friend
has created.

His frustration was forgotten by the visit to East Berlin next
Saturday. Through Checkpoint Charlie, of course. There, he
was shocked by the awful procedure to enter East Berlin. First,
the long wait in a very long queue of people. Then the

embarrassing checking of his identity. Then the forced change of at least 20 western DM to East German Marks.
Then, a long march through deserted streets to the Alexanderplatz. All that is worth mentioning is this: Through a half-opened sewer manhole, a helmet emerges. With a soldier underneath. With field glasses directed at the few pedestrians passing by. And a menacing ready to use machine gun also directed at innocent people,

The 'Alexanderplatz' was gigantic. But just as empty as the streets before. Tedious boring. No open shops. He would have liked to buy chocolate, a newspaper, a souvenir, or at least a picture postcard. No chance at all. He was hungry for a hamburger and even thirstier for beer.
So, the only thing to do was to go immediately back to the much busier 'Kurfürstendamm' as soon as possible.

But now appeared a small glimmer of hope to get rid of the East Marks. In the back of a well-maintained, beautiful park was a kind of small baroque-style castle. Even with light and people in it. Must be very private.

It was not!

It was public because the door could be opened. Going inside he could see a very elegant, very classic, very impressively furnished concert hall. Johann Sebastian Bach could have worked there.

And Bach was what he heard now. A chamber orchestra with over ten black-dressed men and women played it skillfully. His first thought was: "Wow, this must be a very expensive place!"

It was not!

A waiter with a poker face and with astonished eyes led him to a chair at a free table. The prices on the menu card were more than modest for such an establishment. But there was no big choice. To eat was nothing there. But a coffee with vodka for four marks. That was music. And the music got better the more he drank coffee. And, of course, also vodka. What else should he do with his East-Mark?

It became evening. His 'residence permit' in East Berlin will expire very soon. So, he stumbled back to the checkpoint. The procedure to leave East Berlin runs over smoothly.

59.Berlin, Checkpoint Carlie.   **60. Berlin, Alexanderplatz**

7.8. Vienna, Austria.

History is repeating. There is nothing new under the sun.
In Vienna was a machine of the first Supercomputer-Generation installed.
And which also produced again one of the famous software bugs. An error with the so-called 'warm start' feature. After a 'crash' of the OS, this function enabled the previous state to be restored without setting everything to zero. This meant that all active programs do not have to be restarted from the beginning. The warm-start feature was a huge step forward and a great help. And this help did not work anymore in Vienna. Only there. Nowhere else in the world. He was called to Vienna to help his colleague. They knew each other from the time they were in training together in Berlin.
And he was able to help. Relatively soon. This colleague, like himself a software engineer, had made local changes to the OS. It was immediately clear to him, that the dog must have been buried there because it only occurs here.

116

The problem was reproducible and will therefore soon be solved. Once more, Murphy's Law: "If something can go wrong, it will". This was proved once more. This time, for a change, it did not go wrong for him. He found the 'bug'.
More enjoyable was what followed. As it is usual among colleagues, the one who is responsible for a bug pays for a round of drinks. Where will this take place, at the best in the capital of Austria? Of course, in a 'Heurigen' in Grinzing. He and two other colleagues went straight there after work.
Where the 'party', logically, got soon out of hand. In the form of an alcohol level well above one milliliter per one-liter blood.
It was excellent for an immediate sleep in the noble hotel. But not at all good for a night of deep sleep. Because, shortly after midnight, the whole room shook terribly. At first, he thought: "Blame yourself! Drink even more!"
This was not the cause. In Friaul in nearby northern Italy, the earth trembled very violently that night. Much stronger than the one he 'survived' in Sunnyvale.

61. Vienna, Grinzing.

7.9. Ljubljana, Yugoslavia.

After Vienna, he had to go to Ljubljana. This time not for training or troubleshooting.
But for a very other serious reason: He had to create a 'Benchmark' program. Such programs are made for potential

117

future customers or so-called prospects. So, they could compare the different eligible suppliers by measuring their performance. He got a meaningful task. CDC Switzerland was deeply in financial problems and needed badly to sell something.

ETH Zurich had the need and the money to buy a computer for its library. The requirements were as follows: Very fast response time for the user of the library when they were searching for a book, a journal, graphics, and so on.

A CDC computer to meet the challenge and had about the price ETH was willing to pay was not existing in Switzerland. But, what was very seldom the case, the University in Ljubljana had such a machine and had also free capacity. Their machine was exactly the model suitable for the hopefully new deal. And the East-Block state could need the Swiss Francs which CDC Switzerland had to pay.

So, go to Slovenia! This was at that time still part of Yugoslavia.

In a once more stormy flight. This time with the destination Zagreb. With 30 kilograms of manuals in the luggage. To the East-Bloc countries, you had to bring along all the materials which might be needed. And with computers, you never knew what questions and complications will creep up.

The first 'complications' came immediately into the control of the customs officials. They were extremely surprised by the mass of literature. And soon they were overwhelmed. This brought him hours of waiting. The telephones to Belgrade and probably also to the Yugoslavian embassy in Bern run hot. After a thorough inspection of the material, he was unfriendly waved through, and was allowed to enter the country.

The accommodation and the food in Ljubljana brought no pleasure. He had to sleep and eat in a state-run, poorly heated hotel. In a small room with a more or less lousy bed.

But to work at the University was a pleasure. No hustle and bustle, no stress, and everything in peace. Most of the time, he was alone with his friend: The computer.

In the hotel, the variety of the meals was very limited. Even

with the very long, but already somewhat yellowed menu list which contained all the usual in international hotels served 'goodies'. But when he wanted to order something listed on the card, then the always unfriendly waiter said: "We do not have this today". And: "That and most of the others we don't have either".
After two days, he only asked the waiter: "What do you have today?"

After the first two weeks, he had a weekend at home in Geneva.
Back in Zagreb late Sunday evenings, he had to drive with a rented car to Ljubljana. On a bumpy main road with slowly creeping trucks and tight curves. He heard suddenly a muffled, soft bang coming from the front of the car. And he believed to hear a noise as if something fell out of the car and rolled into the bushes.
No panic, then the engine runs fine and the brakes still worked. What he immediately tested.

But this 'bang' became a horrible omen for what was coming very soon. On Monday morning, he wanted to drive to work as usual.

He wanted to!

The engine of the car didn't start! Even the now much more friendly waiter did not manage to get the car going. So, he had to take a cab to go to work. There he called the rental company and asked for help. After work, a car mechanic arrived. The man opened the cooler hood. The man's face got outraged, and he shouted at him: "What happened? What have you done? The starter engine is gone!"
He immediately remembered the bang from yesterday. Everything became clear to him. Not for the mechanic. He listened very skeptically to the story of yesterday's incident. It needed quite a while until the helper believed what he reported. And only because he showed him the three broken bolts on which the starter motor was once mounted. Only later, he learned that stealing parts out of a car was very usual in

the East-Bloc countries.

Quote: "A misfortune rarely comes alone".

The misfortune which must follow was far more embarrassing for him. The day to demonstrate the benchmark program arrived. Three experts from ETH Zurich came to test and review what he had put together.

Oh, fright!

His program does not work at all as it should. They immediately detected a rather big error.
How ashamed he became!
He would have liked to disappear from the earth!

The experts from ETH were, to say the least, not pleased with the results. Everybody went back to Switzerland. So, also the 30 kilos of untouched paper.

And, the bad end of the 'story': ETH did not buy the computer from CDC.

62. Ljubljana, University

8. The 'Grounding' of a Giant. (1978-1982)

8.1. UBISCO.

A repetition of a quotation: "A crisis never comes alone".
The next one was a much more dramatic disaster than the
catastrophic Benchmark, which was partially caused by him.
The next and very drastic flop was clearly not his fault

It was the UBISCO (Union Bank Informatics/Control Data)
project!
He was not involved in the gigantic 'illusion'. A huge bank in
Switzerland and CDC signed a joint agreement to develop
them for the bank required hard- and software. The intention of
the bank was to use for their entire needs only computers from
the same manufacturer. A very colossal challenge for CDC.
The 'deal' was in the order of many millions of dollars. The
existing software was far away to be ready to be used. And it
never will. CDC sold the bank a so-called 'paper tiger'. A term
used in computer business jargon for something that only
exists on paper. In the past, the 'enemy' IBM was often
accused to do this.
The machines of the CDC's 6000d series were extremely
unsuitable for commercial applications. Seymour Cray was
fully aware of this. But not the 'clever' Swiss salesmen and the
management of CDC Switzerland.
The project UBISCO based on the promised TOOS
(Transaction Oriented Operating System) was from the
beginning doomed to fail. With gigantic effort, enormous costs,
and never-ending complications resulted in a fiasco.
Created, most likely in the hell. And In California and Zurich. A
new version of the 'cabbage' was flown to Switzerland once a
week. Accompanied by one of the specialists. Or even by a
more or less pretty secretary who also once wanted to visit
Zurich.

There everybody was for a long time in a very much
unmotivated euphoria. CDC Switzerland gave a huge party. All
employees in Switzerland were invited. Even those in Geneva.

Also, he and his family, too. So, about 120 employees. And everybody with partners, and when they had, children. It took place in a well-known castle in the center of Switzerland. The participants arrived in reserved SBB (Schweizerische Bundesbahn = Swiss national trains) first-class wagons. With champagne breakfast included. After arriving at the hotels, the children were taken care of immediately by hostesses and servants. The boys and girls were not seen anymore until the next day.

The celebration itself took place in the feudal old castle-like building. There the guests were welcomed by fanfares, blown by medieval costumed, professional wind instrument players. The dinner, of course, was the finest of the fine. Accompanied by Vivaldi, played by a small chamber orchestra. Then, of course as usual at such events, endless speeches or better, also, as usual, self praises. Loud applause after each of the 'palavers. For him, these speeches were rather boring and tiring. Everybody was in a great mood. There was jubilation, joy, and cheerfulness. And all were enthusiastic and satisfied with what was offered.

Quote: "Arrogance comes before the fall".

And the fall came soon. The whole UBISCO project collapsed. Crashed into rubble and ashes! This was since a long time written in the sky. An end with horror. Just a little better than an endless horror. The reason why? In his humble opinion: As said, the CDC 6000 serial machines were not built for commercial applications. They don't have instructions that process single characters. Byte-oriented in/output was not possible. The 6000 series machines needed, for efficient interactive use of the CPU, specialized front-end computers. And the ones from CDC were far away from being capable to accomplish the very demanding response-time requirements.

Quote: "Except for expenses, there was nothing"

And those expenses were huge. According to rumors, fifty million Swiss francs. For both, CDC and the bank. He does not know if these figures include the logically following costs for lawyers and tribunals. To the detriment of technology historians, the bank still keeps the files of the UBISCO project under key and lock until today.

8.2. More Catastrophes followed.

Back at CERN. There they had bought a CDC 7600. The successor of the 6600. Even more compact, even denser modules. Now with small flat but still concrete transistors. 4x4 mm square-shaped and one millimeter thick. With switching times of less than one nanosecond. And there were over half a million of those.
He no longer had to repair the new machine. He was now a 'Supercomputer softy'.
But he had nothing to do with the software for the 7600. Fortunately, because of the existing operating system, SCOPE did never run properly.
Another disaster, this time not a technical one, came soon. As said, such disasters do rarely come alone. It happened at CERN. Not much later, hit it the already by the time UBISCO disaster badly shock Swiss branch of the once leading supercomputer company.
CERN did not buy the second 7600. This was so long-waited and hoped for. And was financially terribly needed.
CERN bought an NEC (Nippon Electronic Corporation).
Quote from a Swedish colleague: "The 'shit' hit the ventilator"
Sorry for the wording, but it was the right quote at the right time.
The once glorious company was moving downhill faster and faster. And steeper. Staggering flops like UBISCO, the OS of the 'nuts' SIPROS, PLATO (Programmed Logic for Automatic Teaching Operations) a futuristic project of an electronic schooling system pampered by the founder and CEO of CDC William C. Norris,,and other management failures shoveled her grave. In addition, the catastrophic flop of the 'most super' of all supercomputers. It never saw the light of the real world: The STAR.
Seymour Cray left the sinking ship. While working on the CDC8600. Which never reached the market under this name.

But now was started the advent of something very interesting and new under the sun: The CRAY RESEARCH in Denver, Colorado.

CERN 'forgot' CDC. Only a minimal number of service personnel was still needed. He was completely superfluous.

63. CDC 7600

64. NEC Supercomputer

65. CDC STAR

66. Cray-1

8.3. DIOGENE.

He was completely useless at CERN. After 12 Years. He was feeling to have lost his trousers.
So, what could they do with him? No future customer was in

sight. So, no opportunity to write again a faulty benchmark program. This time, it would have resulted in his being chased immediately to hell.

But if possible, they had to use him somewhere. And hopefully useful. He was still a long way away from the age of retirement. And after all the years, he became a well-paid senior analyst.

There was a gap! Thanks to the never-emerging TOOS OS.

The University Hospital in Geneva had bought, a CDC. The deciding factor why they choose CDC was the TOOS OS. This was, as mentioned before, not the only big flop by CDC over the last few years. And finally, was CDC at that time not the third-largest computer company in the world?

As compensation for non-compliance with the contract, the hospital and CDC agreed as follows: CDC will provide qualified programmers for a longer period. To help to create for the hospital a working system without TOOS.

The personnel at the hospital were working hard and skillfully on their project DIOGENE (Department Informatique Opital Cantonale Geneve). This was a system to optimize the bed occupation, the efficient use of expensive medical equipment, the utilization of medical specialists, general coordination, and so on.

He was quickly integrated into the team. His job: To ensure the backup of the data. He had to program several thousand lines of code in ASSEMBLER. And, of course, night work again. The workplace was not the most convenient. His colleagues and his boss and the biggest boss, a professor, were very friendly and helpful.

It was a rather good place to work. Even if he did not really enjoy writing such a code.

Public transport in Geneva, at that time, was even less fun. Commuting daily from Meyrin to the hospital on the other side of the city by bus with changing lines three times was more than tedious. He was spoiled by the very short way he had from his home to CERN. And where he had a guaranteed parking space.

The DIOGENE project, as a great exception among greater software projects, was completed on time and in good working order. An exception that confirms the famous quote: "The exception proves the rule". And it worked to the entire satisfaction of their users. After all, that's all that matters. What it had cost was only of minor matter.

The project DIOGENE was complete.

His future with CDC was not at all a minor matter. There was, in fact, no future.
He was 'shifted' to the small CDC agency in Lausanne.
This makes the way to work even much more tedious.

The months until it became a fact that CDC falls apart can now be counted on one hand.

And therefore also the end of his very long time with CDC.
And this after 17 years!

9. PR1ME. (1981-1991)

9.1. PR1ME. The 'Epoch' of the Super-Minis.

It is now the beginning of the extinction of the computer 'dinosaurs'. There are still some creations by Cray coming. And the Japanese also began to produce high-tech supercomputers. CERN and ETH bought an NEC.
But now the time of the 'Super-Minis' was coming. He had heard the complaints of his salesmen colleagues: "The Super-Minis are breaking our necks. CDC has to make something which can compete with the newcomers like, for example, DEC (Digital Computer Corporation), PR1ME or others".
PR1ME's computers came close to the performance of the giants for a fraction of the price. When it came to data communication and computer networks, PR1ME was highly more advanced than CDC. In the capability to connect machines from different manufacturers with one another, PR1ME was also superior to CDC.
The salesman who was responsible for a critical existing CDC customer, a leading machine manufacturer in Winterthur near Zurich, told him: "Have a look what PR1ME can do!"

And they can really do a lot better than CDC! He was soon himself convinced of this.

In a Geneva newspaper, a company located in Zurich, which sold PR1ME computers, was looking for software specialists. A phone to Zurich was enough. He got immediately an invitation for a job interview.
At first, their products were presented and demonstrated. He was deeply impressed by their achievements. Even the newly emerging sensational module-oriented computer language PASCAL had already been successfully implemented. This was not so common in the computer world.
By the way: PASCAL was created by Prof. Nicklaus Wirth at the ETH in Zurich.

The connection of monitors, which were still very 'primitive' at the time, to accomplish the interactive use of the central computer was ingeniously simple. Today, they are called client-server connections. It was not to compare to what he had seen until now.

Not so simple was to 'digest' the financial side of the Job they offered him. It was about two thousand Swiss francs a month less than what he earned at CDC. But there was a bonus option. If the company makes a profit in Switzerland, then the employees participate in it. It was unfamiliar to him. So far, only the salespeople have received such a bonus.

But something else was worth much more. They would be happy if he would take over the responsibility for the software and support the entire upcoming complex of data transmission products in western Switzerland.

Difficult to accept was the practical and real pragmatic task in his new job. After a short training session in Zurich, he was, once more, thrown into the cold water. Customer support in western Switzerland was for a long time neglected. It was the highest time to catch up and correct this. Only, the circle of customers was entirely different from the one he was used to. There were among others: A well-known local French bank, a huge retail company in Lausanne, a company in an international global logistic business in Fribourg, the IATA (International Air Transport Association) in Geneva, and also the College Calvin in Geneva.

Then a whole number of small ones. For example, a dairy company in the canton of Valais. A small machine was just sold there. He had to bring their staff, which were cheesemaker, milk dealer, and auxiliary accountant, closer to the computer. Sometimes also in French. It was a truly useless 'exercise'. They were not very interested, and they had a hard time understanding what computers are all about.

But every beginning is difficult. He must have done his work to the full satisfaction of his local boss. This 'Monsieur' was not really his superior but, in fact, 'only' the chief of the marketing representatives. This man must have been very astonished to see the knowledge of the newcomer because he was immediately promoted to Software Manager, Western Switzerland.

The business was booming. One person alone could not cope with the many new installations which were ordered and had soon to be installed. He was told by the highest software boss in Zurich to urgently look for new personnel.

Something he didn't like. But in an emergency eats the devil flies And he did what he was told to do.

Soon the stock of 'softies' in western Switzerland rose from zero to three. That helped...

9.2. 'Kick-Off' in a Château at the Loire.

The new employer's personnel policy was fine. At the beginning of the New Year, he was only with PR1ME for three months, he could take part in the so-called 'kick off' event. Such events were in American companies a habit at the beginning of a new business year in order to motivate the employees to the highest possible mood and to lift their expectations and their happiness hormone levels into the sky. Costs? No questions because PR1ME was doing extremely well.

From Geneva, he and the boss of the salesmen were invited. From Paris, it went to the Loire. In a reserved wagon in a TGV train. They were quartered in a 'Château' next to the named river. And, as it is the habit in a 'Château' at the Loire, immediately 'entertained' with Beaujolais. The wine 'accompanied' them the entire weekend. It nearly ran them out of the ears. So to speak. This made the whole 'exercise' a little more bearable. Because the many hymns of the success of the company, the patting of each other shoulders, and the repetitive: "We are the best" were not necessarily to his 'taste'. Many designers from the company's headquarters in Natick, Massachusetts were there to present their latest 'crimes', say software. The company's marketing consultants were much better than those. The boss responsible for the future

129

development of the PRIMOS operating system was somewhat sticky. He, the Swiss newcomer, asked the 'guru': "What does PR1ME think of UNIX? (Uniplexed Information and Computing System)". For this question, he was nearly killed by the participants. The developer's answer was lapidary: "Do you know a better operating system than our PRIMOS?"
The question of the little Swiss must have insulted the speaker, then the guy did not speak to him during the whole weekend.
The question for UNIX was a call into the desert. Today, he is (almost) sure: If PR1ME had implemented UNIX, the company would have at least survived longer

After the event 'Château at the Loire', other positive news arrived: The birth of PR1ME Switzerland. He got to know only now that PR1ME Computer Switzerland, until then, did not even exist. The computers were sold by a branch of a Swiss investor company, the Trans-KB. A company that was far away from being beyond doubts. It was a company at speculated with the emerging new and highest performing computers. And with the new applications for the pharmaceutics and the machinery industry.
But the PR1ME headquarters in Natick hadn't fallen on the heads. They decided to take over the business in Switzerland themselves: PR1ME Switzerland was founded. This also meant changes to the staff. Not all 'rotten eggs' were taken over by PR1ME. For example, the always phlegmatic junior sales representative in Geneva had to 'take his hat'.
He survived the switch from the bonus-based salary system to real wages. And he felt much better now. And he was used to dealing with an American employer.

The first programs to create technical drawings came to the market and started to conquer the world: The CAD/CAM (Computer-Aided Design/Computer-Aided Manufacturing) applications. The CAD/CAM. software also seemed to be of the highest interest for speculating investors.
CAD/CAM played later a recessive role in PR1ME's history. It turned out later to be a rather sad story.

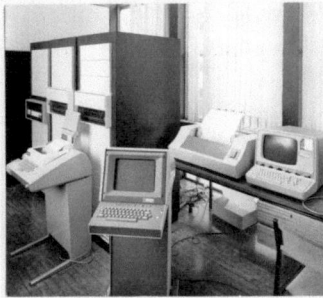

67. Château at the Loire

68. PR1ME 300

9.3. PR1ME at the time they were a leader.

Soon it came clear to him that he now works for a leader in the industry.

But, of course, there was more than only one 'construction site' in the existing installation in Switzerland. For such a one, he was asked by the top software manager in Zurich to go to Bern. In one of the several federal institutes which used PR1ME. He had to help the 'softies' from Zurich, which were responsible for the Bern region, to solve an apparently tricky problem. Although, he came only recently in the contact with the PRIMOS OS.

But soon the problem seemed to be familiar. After installing a new release of the OS, there was a big problem. An application program no longer worked.

This program controlled a rather modest monochrome monitor. That was, as already mentioned, a television set with a keyboard. It is connected to the Super-Mini with twisted paired copper wires.

Studying the source code of the OS was the order of the day. It was written in SIMPLE. This was: kind of assembly language developed al PR1ME for its servers. Such a computer language was not entirely new to him, and it was therefore relatively easy to analyze the error. A tiny little correction was necessary.

Said and done!
And the application was running correctly again. Bright astonishment from the customer, who said: "This man is almost a genius". Which he was surely not. He only had a lot more experience than his younger colleagues. And he was not the first time confronted with such a situation. A system programmer, who recently left the company, made a local modification which was needed to drive the special monitor. The man did an among programmers mortal sin: Not to leave any documentation.

PR1ME had created them for that time unusual and unique programming tool INFO and FORM. These tools made it easy to write interactive business applications. The masks for the monitors for the input and output of the data can be created rapidly. The organization of the required databases was really oriented towards their users, and it is also effortless to control. A chief analyst at the above-mentioned important customer in the retail trade business once said to him: "With INFO and FORM we work three times more efficiently than with COBOL!"

It was a pleasure to listen to the Super-Mini while testing a program. Correctly read: To hear the program. The bits 'whizzing' in the main register is transformed into audible tunes and sent to a loudspeaker. So, he could hear immediately when the program was in a 'loop'. It was much better than the starting of Microsoft Windows today. If their start falls into a loop, you hear nothing. You have to sit in front of the screen and look closely. If the symbols don't move or there is nothing at all to see on the screen, then the start of the PC 'went into the bushes'. (German expression if something drastically fails). Microsoft programs can loop, too. More than the user likes it.

Another big advantage of PR1ME was its prices and flexibility when it comes to upgrades. A customer, a stainless-steel wholesaler, told him that. It only takes an hour to add more megabytes of memory. With IBM machines, it would at least need a night shift. The German-speaking computer specialists translated IBM as: "Immer bis Mitternacht (always until midnight)". Or: "Ich bin müde (I am tired)".

By the way, Burroughs, Remington Rand, CDC, DEC, PR1ME, and many more do no longer exist in the form of a computer pioneer. IBM is still 'in'.

Back to Prime. The price of a storage upgrade was very modest. A French-speaking Swiss customer literally said: "Ca coute deux fois rien". What means:'This costs two times nothing. 'Chapeau'!

Very confidential was the following 'trick' to almost doubling the performance of the CPU. For a not too high price, the maintenance engineer turned a bit on a small switch and 'Whoa': The machine runs much faster. The clock speed was nearly doubled. The machine was from the beginning built to run at higher speed.

No comments!

9.4. Analyst of the year.

He soon got also a 'chapeau'. PR1ME Switzerland chose him as the 'Analyst of the year'. This meant that he could join the three days event in Florida. He was promoted to a member of the 'Hundred percent club'. In this club, there were mostly the salesmen who had accomplished 100 percent of their predicted sales figures.

The 'Thanksgiving' was not as convenient as the one in the euphoric heydays of the CDC. He had to sleep in a double room together with a very unfriendly guy from Sweden. They did not speak to each other.

But breakfast was formidable. And, of course, with an intensive speech by a vice president. Intended to motivate the audience.

A visit to a nearby Disneyland was more pleasant. With everything included. Much to the delight of the much younger participants. Not for him. Only the three-dimensional movies in big tents did excite him.

Not so 'high-tech' was in Disneyland the public telephone service. Respectively, it did not exist. There was only the possibility to use one of the open telephone booths. We were still decades away from the time humanity was over floated with mobile telephones.

He had to make an urgent phone call to Switzerland. One of his girlfriends, hopefully eagerly, awaited his call. It was very hot in the telephone cell without a door, and he sweated awfully. There was a bank to get change. There he got half a kilo of 'quarters '. Those are 25 US cents coins. The conversation with Zurich surprisingly took place. A coin must be inserted again after every twenty seconds.

After a large-scale party, more for teenagers than for him, the 'show' in Florida was over. Back to everyday life. With an award in the suitcase. Kind of a trophy. A beautiful round glass panel with a nicely written validation of his achievements packed in an elegant wooden, polished frame

.

69. Award for Analyst of the year 1983

9.5. Rigi-Kaltbad

The next place in the 'The Other Computer History' is Rigi-Kaltbad. And that in November. It was wet, cold, and foggy in the deserted mountain resort. Most of the shops were closed. Most hotels too. But not the one where he was now. It was only scarcely heated, rather unfriendly, and rather miserable. There were no other guests than the participants of the workshop which was now awaiting him. He was one of the 'privileged' who was commanded to attend. All salespeople, marketing managers, senior engineers and senior 'softies' in Switzerland were there. The executive committee consisted of a vice president from Natick with a secretary, a responsible development technician, a psychologist, an actor from the USA, and, of course, all the bosses of PR1ME Switzerland. Unfortunately, also the unpopular human resources manager.

Everything that had to be expected arrived. Exuberant welcome greetings, handing out the usual self-praise and everything else that was common on such occasions.
The next day, hard work started. In groups, they had to study a business case. Until deep into the night, they had to prepare a presentation to be given the next day to the bosses from Natick. Then there was free beer. But don't drink too much, the personnel manager was present, and noticed every glass they drank.
On the other day, one of the groups had to present what the group had worked out. Of course, it 'hits' him. He had no success with his presentation. The jury made up of the present Americans was not at all impressed. The work of the whole group was not appreciated either. There was criticism like: The presentation technique is insufficient. The actor explained why. Lack of self-confidence, lousy facial expressions, faulty language, restlessness, no gestures, and much more. The marketing expert criticized the order of the presentation, the quality of the slides, and the stupid persuasiveness of the lecturer. The designer didn't like the technical side of what was so hardly prepared by the team.
Time for a break. Yes, but don't smoke, the personnel manager was present. After the effort of the presentation, he

had to move his legs a bit. Outside it was bitterly cold. He felt like to do what in German was called: 'Sich verschlaufen'. This is an expression in the Swiss military service if one would like to disappear from the scene.

But here it was anything but recommendable. So, he walked visibly embarrassed through the lecture hall. The entire leadership staff sitting at the back of the room took a break. Probably even a break for smoking...

Accidentally, he went behind their table. And could not help but to take a shy and hopefully unobserved look at what they had scribbled on the papers lying around.

That gave him a cold shiver! He could read very clearly what was written there by the head of personnel. Under the name of the participants, who didn't belong to the staff, the following was written:

Almost falls asleep.
Doesn't listen.
Keeps his legs moving.
Doesn't get involved at all.
Speaks poor English.
Good night!!! Or better, he doesn't wish the personnel manager a good night! This was kindergarten at a higher level!

A cool beer was now very much needed. But the free beer was only available after 2000h. It was cold in Rigi-Kaltbad!

9.6. PR1ME and IBM's SNA.

His memories of Rigi-Kaltbad are also very frosty. Back to Geneva. There he will soon have to apply what he had learned. He had to give a lecture to customers and PR1ME staff in Geneva.

The topic: SNA (Systems Network Architecture). A proprietary collation of data transmission protocols. A creature, of course, by the mighty IBM. The purpose of SNA is to improve the communication between IBM devices and, reluctantly, with the rest of the computer world.

SNA and the many other upcoming telecommunication protocols were urgently needed in the rapidly emerging brand-new epoch of the global networks. SNA was described in a two hundred-page book in complicated, this time IBM specific, computer 'Chinese'.

He had to make his lecture very concentrated and understandable even for laypeople. And of course in English. And here is how it was done: First, check everything important for a presentation. As was learned on the Rigi. Optimal setting of the overhead projector, ensuring the presence of replacement light bulbs, checking the microphone and the amplifier system, control the seating in the hall that everyone has a clear view at him, and to check the optimal lighting of the premises. Everything was perfect. He, as always when he had to give a presentation, was extremely tense. Even a cigar and a glass of white wine beforehand did not help.

Light off. Overhead projector light on. Everybody looked tensely at him. Total silence. He put the first slide on the overhead projector. It did not contain the usual list of issues that will be presented. It was just plain white. And then he quoted: "In the beginning there was nothing. And IBM has seen that there was nothing. And IBM created SNA". He got a roar of laughter for his parable with the Book of Genesis in the Bible. The good mood of the audience was immediately reached. Almost perfect rhetoric. As he just learned in Rigi-Kaltbad.

So far, he had had no problems with SNA. The first trouble with the monstrous design came soon. Nearly as a must. The already mentioned major customer in Ober-Winterthur, like the companies that were technically and financially up to date, used computers from different manufacturers. In addition to IBM, CDC, and DEC, it was also a modest PR1ME there. An important customer application required connections between the giant and the dwarf. The difference in size was only physical.

Thanks to SNA, it has now become possible for the two to 'speak' to each other. And as usual, something like this doesn't work right away. So, again he had to hurry to near Eastern

Switzerland, namely to 'Oberi '(local name for Ober-Winterthur). And it is now the middle of a severe winter.
He was equipped with a brand new and costly tool: The data analyzer. This is an ingenious monitor with which the data running over a wire could be seen in the clear. Secrete's like Bank account numbers, passwords, love letters, porn's, and anything else which is very private could be read crystal clear. A very nice machine for hackers. An expression that did not even exist at that time. And encryption was not very common yet. The data analyzer is a very sophisticated device. It helped him relatively quickly to solve the problem. Because it was reproducible. It was a protocol violation error in the SNA implantation in IBM!

What? There is no such thing! IBM doesn't make mistakes!

It needed his full powers of persuasion and a little over a month until everything was as should be. No word or comment from IBM. He didn't expect it, eider.

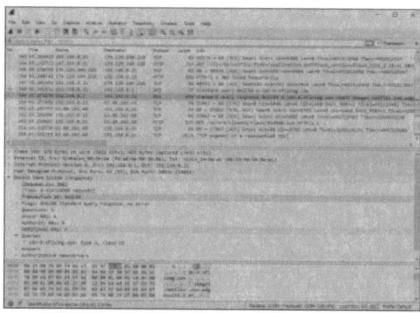

70. Data Analyzer Display

138

9.7. SPUG. Swiss PR1ME user's group.

PR1ME Switzerland urgently needed competent employees. And such were available! Even 'en masse'. Namely, the ex-CDC employees. They left the sinking ship like rats. He was the first one. Soon followed by about a dozen of them. He had prepared the way.

They were much more competent than the man he should now teach in Zurich. He was probably from the Far East. Or, as his boss later put it, an Asian sly dog. The 'chemistry' between the newcomer and him was far away to be the same. He asked him: "What are you most interested in technical literature?" The man replied: "Everything!" So from INFO and FORM to SIMPLE, FORTRAN, COBOL, and PASCAL. From X25 to Token-Ring and from Ethernet to SNA. With a shake of the head, he handed him an approximately 30 cm high pile of manuals.

But the man had never before worked with a computer! Well! "The Lord gives it his in sleep" (Psalm 127.2).

The Asian worked for PR1ME only for a very short time. After the second assignment to help a customer, the guy was immediately dismissed or better 'kicked out'.

This 'case' was also a topic at the next meeting of the SPUG: The Swiss Prime User Group. This was an association of Prime customers. In order to better enforce their wishes, concerns, and complaints and to 'cry out' together.

He was 'punished' to represent the company at this conference. He had to apologize for the capital mistake made by the personnel manager when hiring this man. To accomplish that, he had to invent tedious improvised incomprehensible excuses.

But the far more sensible and bigger problem for customers was this: The PCs are on the rise. They must be connected to the Super-MInI. That was now a 'must'. PR1ME can do this as one of the first mainframe manufacturers. Where also was the problem?

Money! What else! The much-needed new and now hopefully error-free version of the OS PRIMOS did no longer support the older version of Microsoft Windows. It was no longer compatible. In plain language: The customers had to upgrade their PCs. They had to buy a new version of Microsoft Window. A non-budgeted and therefore difficult to digest not expected expense.

9.8. Telecommunication Marketing Manager

Far less cumbersome or even embarrassing than the order to be exposed to angry customers was his promotion to PR1ME Switzerland Telecommunication Marketing Manager. Now, at the beginning of the eighties, the time of computer networks and the Internet really started. PR1ME understood the sign of the time early. In comparison with CDC and also with the unbeatable IBM. PR1ME was, as far as he knows, far ahead of those.
One customer, the College Calvin in Geneva, was a pioneer in this new domain. It received the tenth IP address of those who were assigned to Switzerland. The protocol TCP/IP (Transmission control protocol/internet protocol) and those belonging to the same family had unique success in the history of computer science. Without those, the internet would not exist in the form as it is today!
Switzerland got a contingent of IP addresses assigned. These were managed and distributed by the ETH Zurich. The first address was for ETH. The next ones were for CERN, the College Calvin, and, PR1ME Switzerland. He was proud to work for such a leading company.

And was also proud to participate in the annual PR1ME telecommunication products marketing manager meetings in Massachusetts. There he met colleagues from all over the world. The purpose and aim of this event were to report the needs of the market to those responsible in Natick. To tell them what the customers want. To give the designers
140

feedback on what were the priorities in the real world.
The requirement of the connectivity to IBM was solved by implementing SNA. The most important need was, however, the expansion and improvement of the connections to the increasingly upcoming PCs. Those were more and more replacing the Super-Minis. The market had changed.
The discussions over this theme were fierce. The priorities about what the manufacturer should implement first vary from country to country. With its modest order volumes were the wishes of Switzerland only of minor importance. He defended them and demanded that the interfaces to the output devices for the CAD/CAM application must fully be integrated into the further development of PRIMOS. The computer from PR1ME had the great ability to master the demand of these rapidly growing applications.

The two-week gathering was loosened by casual beer-drinking evenings. Now, they were drinking the in Massachusetts produced 'Samuels' beer. It was, as again proudly emphasized, brewed according to the German beer brewing purity law. The 'Leinenkugel' beer in Chippewa Falls, which he always remembered, was much better. But as it is well known, one can argue about taste. There was also a slight attempt by the Americans to teach the others how to play Baseball. Or better and more exact: Softball. The Europeans then tried in vain to explain to the Americans the 'finesse' of European football (soccer in the US).

On Saturday evening, there was offered a dignified dinner in an elegant restaurant in Boston. With their specialty: The lobster. He brought such animals, still alive, back to Zurich on his return flight. Swissair provided a freezer service free of charge.
Communication with his son, who was still attending primary school in Geneva, is also free. No longer by telephone. That is from now on 'passé'. But via an acoustic coupler in the apartment in Geneva. This was a simple and inexpensive device. The real first-generation PC of his son was connected to it. The network side was established over the ordinary telephone receiver. The only handling that was needed, was to

place the telephone receiver over the acoustic coupler. The data transmission rate was about as fast as that of a teletype, namely a lousy 75 baud. The error rate was just barely bearable.

In Natick, he was able to 'talk' with his son by using the Super-Mini available to the visitors. And, he was able to fulfill his son's request, communicated via the acoustic coupler, to bring home a 1 megabit microchip for his PC. And he also received his wife's 'emailed' order for an artificial Christmas tree with a ten-year guarantee. Such a one was not available in Switzerland.

For the communication, his son did have to be present. Today we say he had not to be online. A term, which just 'crept' up in the IT world, This fact, not to be online was very useful. The time difference between Massachusetts and Geneva is six hours.

It was the preliminary step to what is indispensable in the world today. The E-mail was born. With a Commodore PC of the first generation on a kitchen chair next to the still long used analog telephone.

The first e-mail technology that came up was not the one most in use today: The TCP/IP. Today, every child knows what this is.

The email protocols of the 'X' family were first. Another one of the packet switching transmission protocols. They are also called frame-relay implementations. The electronic mail protocol X400 was in use first. PR1ME, of course, had it, as always, very early implemented. The salesmen proudly showed their X400 addresses on their business cards. To show how advanced PR1ME was.

The series of 'X' protocols have never really prevailed. Why? In his humble opinion because too complicated and because developed by a committee, the former CCITT (Comité Consultatif International Téléphonique et Télégraphique).

X.25 was nevertheless attractive to him. So much that he tried for the first and last time to be a 'hacker'. To realize with horror how easy it was!

He stopped immediately. And never did it again...

71. Acoustic Coupler

9.9. And PR1ME also disappeared.

PR1ME and its biggest competitor, the DEC, soon got a deadly fright: The computer on every office table, in the kitchen, and the barn. What Ken Olson, CEO, and co-founder of DEC, never believed. DEC was at that time number two in the IT business. Just one behind the, of course, untouchable number one: IBM.
DEC was 'swallowed' by COMPAQ. Which later was taken over by Hewlett-Packard. Will HP be digested by Microsoft, Apple, Samsung, or Intel?
In the future, the business of the 'von Neumann' machines will probably be 'thrown' by the Japanese, Chinese, Taiwanese, or companies from India. Certainly, not by Europeans nor by Americans.

He once said to his sons: "Go east, young man. Because there is nothing new in the West".
Derived from the title of the famous novel by Eric Maria Remarque.

Personal computers, laptops, Smartphones, and whatever else will come is in every humble hut today. In Third World countries, often more than bread and butter.

The CEO of PR1ME Joe M. Henson did not buy the MEDUSA CAD/CAM product from ComputerVision for a 'sandwich'. But for an impressive $300 million. Probably cash and not with the now deeply submerged PR1ME stocks. And the dollar was still valued much higher than the Swiss franc.
He got, on a return flight from Boston to Zurich, personally in contact with the highest Boss of PR1ME. Because they had both the same destination: Zurich. The CEO was most likely on his way to Swiss banks. To beg the 'gnomes' there for money?
Joe M. Henson asked him in the airplane: "Did I do right to buy ComputerVision?"

Even not being a professional businessman, he today clearly shouts: NO!

Because it was the beginning of the doom. The evil hit many who were 'blessed' with the company's once sought papers.
He has no good memories of stock securities. He was, not so long ago, also a proud owner of Control Data and PR1ME shares. The employees could buy them at a special price. The number of shares was limited. Luckily! Buying them was something like a 'must'. Otherwise, the loyalty of the employee was in question.
Now they are still usable for wallpapering the walls. He does not pity all the professional speculators and short-term moneymakers when their shares are diving. And those of the PR1ME plunged into the bottomless.
Money makes the world go round. Not the computers. No artificial intelligence (AI) program will be able to change this fact.
Financial geniuses are smarter. One had found out that the value of PR1ME's real estate was worth more than the total capital of the shares. So, the Company was bought up, scrapped, and disassembled. And then the real estate was sold. With huge profit.
The ones who bought it will surely later make more again.

144

10. Between PR1ME and the last job.

10.1. Life goes on.

PR1ME went down the drains. And he with it. He was fired.
Kicked in the ass. Thrown at the street. At the age of over 50.
With a family. With two sons. One of them was still at the
university studying Informatics.

Quote: "The apple falls not far from the trunk".

The other 'PR1ME victims', all younger than him, were also
put on the street. Even those he had brought earlier into the
computer business. That PR1ME had a free fall was not his
'Culpa'. And he did not feel guilty about it either.

His colleagues soon found a job. And started a new career in
the now rapidly emerging companies that took over the legacy
of the Super-Minis. And later, these companies were often
taken over themselves. A recurrent theme in the history of IT.

His colleagues soon found a new job. For example, with:

TANDEM Computers.
SUN.SILICON GRAPHICS INTERNATIONAL (SGI).
NIXDORF ('Nix' in German means 'nothing'. But NIXDORF
was not 'nothing'!).
WANG
HEWLETT PACKARD and others,

WANG was a very successful technology leader founded by
An Wang, a Chinese woman resident in the United States.
They had great success with the international organizations in
Geneva because their computers, as a rough exception and to
his knowledge the only ones who had a rectangular monitor in
portrait format.

Very popular with the secretaries. They can see a sheet on the monitor, as they were used to before the computer age. An A4 page is displayed as such.

 Something else, also quite new, was the connection between the PCs and the servers: A broadband network. This allows TV signals, telephone services, and data transmission to 'run' over the same cable. It is a quite thick coaxial cable. A striking advertising image was this: A well-dressed gentleman said this: Everything over one wire. He was not talking of the need for expensive amplifiers at both ends for this type of network. This technique was also in use by TV channel providers and others like UPC (formerly CABELCOM).

He had no success with these aspiring young 'newcomer' companies. He was too old for them. And the American companies pay child supplements and old-age pension funds only with gnashing of the teeth.

 He had to dig up long, unused job references, write long job applications, turn his thumbs, and drink as little beer as possible. There was not enough money for a humble glass of wine. This might even be better for his health. But giving up smocking the cheapest available cigar he did not achieve. What else was the life worth living for?

He was not frequently called for an interview. Why? He was overqualified. And, up to this point, too well paid. He had throughout knowledge in nearly all the domains of IT. He was multilingual and had now very good references. The customers he was supporting wrote about his excellent job qualifications and recommended him highly to future employers. In vain!

But suddenly, a little shimmer of light appeared. Not necessarily what he was looking for.

Why? The company was part of a Bank! He once swore: I never work for a Bank!
But, as it often happened in life: Resolutions are thrown over the heap.

And as said once before: Money doesn't stink…

10.2. Intermezzo Bank Applications.

But now he came with lots of money into contact. Not with coins. The amounts were closer to the millions. Of course, not his. But for the banks which were customers of the company that offered him a job. Despite his advanced 'Middle Age'. This company was a branch of a Tel Aviv resident software company that pecialized in software packages for money transfers. These were:

SIC, Swiss Interbank Clearing.
SWIFT, Society for Worldwide Interbank Financial Telecommunication.

The Zurich-based branch of this software manufacturer that wrote such applications consisted of four heads. They needed someone else for maintenance, or more exactly, to help to sell their products
Modest wage and again with the promise to share the profits. Those profits, in reality, then never existed.
First, there will be three months training period in Zurich. Later the will provide an office in Geneva. He naively trusted them. It never happened.

But why shouldn't he try? There was not much to lose. In Geneva, he never would have found a job allowing him to 'survive' at the level he was used to.

The office building, where the small Swiss agency of the company in Zurich was located, was very modern. With an aluminum facade, large comfortable halls, long corridors, and spacious, mostly unoccupied bright open offices. The house was most modern. Equipped with the latest building technology. A so-called 'intelligent' construction. Too intelligent for him. Because in April, the sun blinds automatically go down with a noise that could not be ignored. Only to immediately go back up again.

That made him quite nervous. Especially because he now had to help to write a business proposal in French. This required his fullest concentration because his written French was more than poor. In technical matters, however, he was able to produce the required paper.

The (hopefully) next client entirely ignored what he had written.

Again, he didn't have the smallest chance. He was, once more, a complete 'loser'.

So, Geneva did not need a software manager. Immediately he knew that the stage in Zurich will last much longer than announced. And, even worse, Zurich will be his place to work. He is back to his birth down after being almost 30 years away.

Therefore, he had to look for an apartment. Found only a room with was part of the apartment of the landlady. Fortunately, she was more friendly than the one in Eau Claire.

Then he drove the furniture of his son's child's room to Zurich. In his old Ford-Granada station wagon. The rented room did not have a telephone installed. He had to order a telephone line because the use of the recently emerging mobile telephone net was still outrageously expensive.

In the office, there was not much of use to do. Until then, when, he was sent to Paris. There, he had to install for a customer the latest version of the bank application software. Nothing new for him.

The 'trip' had to be as cheap as possible. He was lodged in a modest little building. It was in reality a 'sleazy' hour hotel. And also situated in such a district.

He could walk to the small bank. There he 'sank' two floors below street level. The computer was there for security reasons. Of course, an IBM 'block' that had long passed its expiring dates. That's why the update took endless hours. It started late after 22h00. It was extremely boring. He could not sleep. Because until well beyond midnight, the metros rattled through. Just about three meters behind a shabby, non-plastered damp gray wall.

There was not much rest in the hotel during the day either. Luckily, the whole nightmare was over after two days.

Back in Zurich. A registered blue letter was waiting for him: "Due to the bad business situation, we are unfortunately forced to terminate the employment contract". In German: He got again the shoe in the ass.
 As he found out later, a planned deal with a well-known Zurich bank did not work out. And he was the victim.

Quote: "You shall never sink so low as to drink from the cocoa through which you are pulled!" (Erich Kästner).

So, for the rest of the two months, he survived. How? Looking out the window, emptying wastebaskets, distributing sandwiches, sorting manuals, and other such demanding 'high-tech' tasks.

11. The Networks. (1993-2004)

11.1. The last challenge.

Now, there was again the same horrible situation as twice before. Study newspaper for job offers. Then write job applications, luck at the stars, and hope for a chance. And to make it worse than before: he was now almost two years older.

It is now the time to quote again Maria von Ebner-Eschenbach: "Coincidence is a necessity shrouded in veils". Or for believers: "Coincidence is if the Lord does not want to be seen"

Such a coincidence happened to him once more. For the last time?
This time it was a veil in blue. In the color of IBM. They gave a one-day seminar. Theme: The expected future of developments in the IT world. It was, to repeat it, the 'sunrise' of the Internet. And a future which will completely be conquered by personal computers. And 'big blue' wanted, of course as it was stated many times before, to be at the top of whatever will be coming. And as it should be for IBM: To become the leader.
A seminar given by IBM was for its customers free of charge. So, he could attend it. He was at that time anyway 'out' of useful actions for the software company which just fired him. They were not yet 'out' of business. But very 'wobbly'. And the 'out' will soon a be reality.

The seminar was very professional. The lecturers are in the correct dark blue suit. With the perfect facial expressions, skillful presentation techniques, and even without the IBM song. He was not at all bored. He sat, as usual, in the back row of the seats.

Now someone touched him on the shoulder and said in a friendly voice: "Hi Hans, what are you doing here?" He turned himself abruptly around. He recognized the gentleman at once. It was a colleague from the blessed to unhappy time with CDC. And then later, with the many positive days with DIOGENE.

He had not met him for years. They started a conversation. His friend was working for a well-known important Swiss Financial Institution which was, of course, an excellent and also solvent customer of IBM. He is the group leader of a small group of three people, responsible for the installation and maintenance of the networks.

He told him his own story about his suffering since CDC's downfall and the bankruptcy of PR1ME. And that he just was 'kicked out' by the more than frivolous software maker.

The former colleague listened very intensively. And said: "Man, if I had known that you would work in Zurich, I would have a job for you".

He had!

He was soon offered a newly created post as a telecommunication technician. Without profit sharing or stock options. Wage adjusted to the job requirements, sense of responsibility, education, title, age, language skills, and professional experience.

Which he had, of course, in abundance.

11.2   The Token-Ring and its pitfalls.

He was at the beginning not very comfortable with the new job. An unfamiliar environment for him, who was used to the stress which was common among American and other computer companies. Here, they took it rather easy.
At least until now. His two stage's higher chief, here they were called 'Director', remarked soon: "Not so hotly. You make yourself unpopular"
Soon he was complete 'next to the shoes'. He, who was used to speaking with his work colleagues using the in the German language usual familiar 'DU', was looked at outraged by a member of the staff and reaps an evil eye. Because the guy had an academic title on his business card.

He was very proud to work for such an enterprise. The Institution was generally not exactly up-to-date with computer networks. And extremely IBM-oriented. If not dependent.
The PCs and printers, distributed across various buildings, were linked to the mainframes using the 'Token-Ring' technology. Most of the buildings were old. This did not simplify the installation of the now-required fiber optic cables.
Several such Token-Ring LANs (Local Area Networks) in different buildings were interconnected with such cables. They were very delicate to maintain. To work with the fiber optic connectors was only allowed by technicians specially trained for this. At that time, the rental fee of these fiber-optic cables was still in an astronomical range.
If the ring was interrupted somewhere, then nothing works at all. The same was the case if one of the network interfaces of a connected device did not work as should. This caused the collapse of the whole ring.

As was soon proved by a serious problem. The emergency power supplies for all the buildings must be checked every month. This required a very brief interruption of the network. And now came the big new 'evil': Nothing works after the restart.

Alert level one!

He knows what to do. Attach the data monitor, and observe closely what is happening or what is not happening. If a device is connected to the Token-Ring, then it had first to ask for the so-called parameter server. This is a kind of chief machine in the ring that passes the parameters relevant to this particular local network to the connected devices. This function was usually performed by a router. In the now so problematic case, a 'vulgar' user PC performed this function.
And wrong! As it turned out later, caused by an unfortunate series of components in a PC in combination with a certain version of Microsoft Windows. It needed again his fullest conviction power to prove this to the others. A specialist from Microsoft was called. The man was able to reproduce the problem, and therefore he could repair it.
Question: Does Microsoft make errors?

72. IBM Token-Ring MAU   **73. Token-Ring Connector**

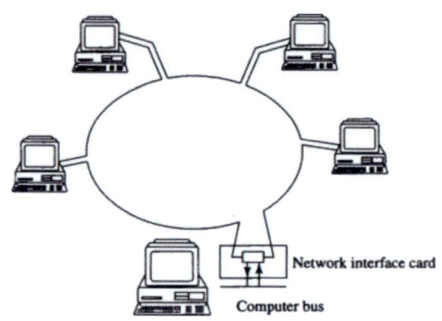

Network interface card

Computer bus

74. Token-Ring Architecture

11.3. The Ethernet.

The network connection technology that was better known to him was the Ethernet. The organization IEEE, the Institute of Electrical and Electronics Engineers, specifies Ethernet in the 802.3 protocols. Its maintenance and installation are much easier than for the Token-Ring.

Where the name Ethernet does come from? It is not, as so usual with computer terms, an abbreviation. It has something to do with 'ether'. Digital signals were sent over the air in the Aloha radio net in Hawaii in 1970. This net inspired Mr. Robert Metcalfe in the Xerox Palo Alto Research Center (PARC) lab to design the Ethernet LAN protocol. The whole Ethernet system is based on CSMA/CD (Carrier Sense Multiple Access / Collision Detection) technologies.

It became one of the biggest successes in IT.

At the beginning of this technology, it was not a network but 'just' a thick yellow insulated cable up to 150 meters long. To it, the devices were connected. Simple: With a special tool, a hole was drilled through the insulation of the cable to the copper conductor. Then, the wire from the device that had to be added to the net is plugged in. And the device is immediately connected.

The various types of LANs could be explained as follows: At the beginning of the time when simple Monitors, PCs, Printers, and similar devices were connected to a computer, each device had a simple copper cable to the host. It was the so-called 'star' method.

A 'parable': He compares the different technologies used in the LANs with existing political systems. The star approach is a dictatorship. The host queries each device in a programmed rhythm (polling). The Token-Ring system is a democracy. Each device in the LAN comes to 'word'. Another prominent name is, in American terms, the 'daisy chain' (milkmaid's chain): The milkmaid goes from one little house to the next one. Ethernet is chaos. To compare with the 'regulars' table in a pub. Every participant chats uncoordinated. The one that roars the loudest But Ethernet is, as said, the LAN technique that had the widest success.

75. Robert Metcalve, Ethernet Pioneer

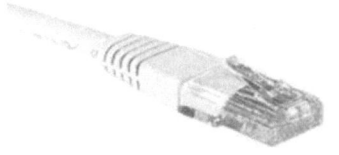 

76. Ethernet Connector   **77. Ehternet Cable.t**

11.4. CICSO.

The challenge to connect the different LANs to each other was obvious. The required adaption must be done somewhere. And this was badly needed because, as mentioned, many times before, the technically very demanding internet has started with full speed to conquer the world.

The most important new generation of devices that made the internet possible is the ROUTER. Like the name says: It routes the data packets through the network. Not only that. It also was able to process and convert different protocols.

The 'advent' of a tremendous interesting machine, namely the router, arrived.

The most known was designed in 1986 by Bill Yeager from Stanford University and then implemented and improved by Len Bosack and Sandy Lerner from CISCO Corporation. The name is based on the company's location: San Francisco. The corporate emblem was, until 2006, the Golden Gate Bridge, the famous suspension bridge to the entrance to the San Francisco Bay. The company had fantastic success, and this is still true today: Without CISCO, no Internet. The company had once, for a short time, the highest market value of all the companies worldwide, proudly 555 billion dollars.

But also the CISCO routers were not without problems.

It was expected and it arrived. So sure, like the 'Amen' in the church.
There were and there still are network breakdowns caused by routers. CISCO was not immune to those.
 distribution room, he sat on the rickety stool. He made his first attempt to configure a router. It was already one of the second generations, a CISCO 4000. In a beautiful dark blue. In the color of the company's emblem. This model was no longer in the ugly mouse gray-orange like the first router from CISCO, the AGS (Advanced Gateway System).
What was not so nice was what happened now. A slight bang. A fine black smoke appeared, and it started to stink.
It also 'stinks' him. The beautiful new device was in the bucket. The power supply unit had exploded. The power supplies in general, the accumulators, and the batteries are still today one of the weak points in routers, PCs, laptops, modern Smartphones, and so on. And to whatever will still come one day.
A not-so-easy-to-diagnose problem followed. This time again a hardware failure. All specialists were for a week not at their normal place of work. A workshop had taken place somewhere in the near mountains. The next generation of the network had to be planned. The participants did not want to get disturbed by everyday questions and problems.
All specialists were away and clearly, it happened exactly then. As usual, at the worst possible time. The data traffic between the main building and the computer center at the other end of town was in lousy shape.

He also!

He had as speedy as possible to take a cab to Zurich. There he immediately installed the 'sniffer' (the jargon word for the network data stream analyzer). And then very hard work was needed. The problem was, as the devil wanted, not reproducible.
In such a case, only intuition and practical experience help. And that was to replace in the AGS router one after the other

157

of all the possible components which could have caused the failure.

After every change, look up to the sky, pray and hope for a wonder to come. These replacements were very labor-intensive and stressed the nerves. Of course, this had to be done at night. After the fourth attempt, it seemed to be repaired, then for two days, everything was again working as usual. The last printed circuit card replaced which contained hundreds of the smallest microchips caused most likely the highly delicate and very cumbersome problem.

The router software was not always beyond any doubt. It matured also, as has been mentioned so often, on the customer side. The famous CISCO was no exception. That will soon be proofed.

The computer center in Zurich was connected to the branch offices by leased copper wires. A capacity like the one in optical fiber cable was not required. And telephone leased lines are more flexible, bendable, and much cheaper. This wire connection must be managed with additional technical resources. And also requires a backup connection. This was accomplished by using the ISDN (Integrated Services Digital Network) service of Swisscom. Or was it still PTT?

Data can by means of a modem (modulator/demodulator) be transmitted over a normal telephone cable. The bandwidth is however quite modest.

The Institution paid him such a connection to his apartment. For the on-call duty. In the event of a breakdown of the network, he had to be able to intervene from home.

If business data is sent over the public ground, it must be encrypted. Because most money is involved. Even lots of money! This was a very strict regulation given from them for the security responsible chief, the Security Officer. CISCO routers are themselves able to perform encryption. And this over the ISDN protocol.

You might think!

He tried for weeks to make it work. Somehow something always went wrong. He was told by his colleagues: "This is your problem. You simply cannot configure the device correctly".

It was not so!

The called in responsible certified CISCO engineer finally had to concede: A software problem in the router. Certain segments of a message were simply sent in clear. In the Bible, it would be written as a new commandment: "Thou shall not send certain segments in the clear".

So, as a reward for his patience with the routers, he was invited twice by CISCO to the annually held major event. Offered generously by CISCO to their customers. With pomp and ceremonies in Monaco and Copenhagen. With lectures, seminars, and gala dinners. And, of course, free beer.

78. CISCO AGS Router   **79. CISCO Emblem**

11.5. The WAN (Wide Area Network).

His employer builds a closed data network throughout
Switzerland. Using the most advanced techniques. And the
most modern routers. They are connected to each other by
fiber optic cables. The network is designed in such a way that
a break of one fiber optic line does not interrupt the
functionality of the entire net. The regulation requires that
there is no single point of failure which could cause the
network to collapse. All the connections must be designed so
that they don't follow the same geographical way and do not
use the same amplifier. Inside the buildings, they must run
over different shafts. The equipments for the two lines were
not allowed to be in the same room.
Fiber optic connections over a longer distance became only
now in use everywhere. His prognosis: "In the not so distant
future there will be fiber optic cables to every office table" was
commented by his colleagues with roaring laughter.
Today, January 2021, he has fiber optic cable to his modest
one-room apartment at an affordable price and with a
throughput capacity of one gigabit
And fiber optic cables have become more flexible. The first
version had the handicap of a limited radius when they had to
be bent.
He is now a TCS. That means a telecommunication specialist.
He proudly shows this title on his business card to everybody.
He is no longer 'only' a network technician. But that also
required a good portion more responsibility. Because as soon
as something goes wrong, even very locally, the devil is in the
house. Not to mention what he calls in German A GNAU
(Grosser Netzwerk Ausfall = Big Network Collapse). Or even
worse! A UNGNAU. An expression invented by him. It stands
for 'Unspunnen grosser Netzwerkausfall'. It is derived from the
big 83.3 kilograms heavy 'Unspunnenstein' which is in the
yearly festival pushed into the sand by heavy athletes. This
takes place in Interlaken. A city in the Swiss Alps.

He is shuddering at the thought of a possible global collapse

of the Internet. Will he experience one? He certainly doesn't hope so.
But one of such medium-size 'world doom' will surely arrive one day.

11.6. The Encryption 'Monster'.

Now, a Swiss company was finally coming into play. The Swiss low-voltage industry has not completely 'overslept' the modern time. We are talking about a company that produces encryption devices. They don't build computers or routers. But something that is becoming increasingly important, and badly needed in the upcoming, until now, unbelievable, worldwide 'storm' caused by the internet.
Earlier, a company in Regensdorf/ZH had constructed such encryption machines. Mostly mechanical and very noisy devices packed in bullet-proven steel boxes. Mainly used in the Swiss army. The company was then later, but not because of its business with such encryption devices, going bankrupt. The reason was, once more, a technical flop: The Eidophor. But this doesn't really belong in the context here.
Fortunately, a company not far from Zurich builds encryption devices for the highest demands: Transmission rates in the gigabit range over fiber optic cables. These are now urgently needed by his Institution. And were, of course, costly

And, to his astonishment, they worked very well. For once, not the 'tropical fruit syndrome'? Is it really an exception?
No!
An encryption device had very sporadically a failure.
Fortunately, only for a very short time. It corrected itself by a restart. This was not noticed by the normal network user. After all, the network was, he repeats it again, built redundantly. But the network technicians noticed it quickly. They were very distressed.
By now, there are over half a dozen telecommunication specialists employed by the Institution. But no one of his colleagues was able to reproduce the problem.

161

He could!

He was able to do it. But, of course, not during normal production hours. His boss would have killed him. At first, no one believed him. But he proved it. If he applied a so-called 'SNMP request' from his PC, the 'gigabit mixer' starts to 'skid'. SNMP stands for Simple Network Management Protocol. And it's simple. Created by a few geniuses who invented the simple TCP/IP protocols. According to the rumors, SNMP was developed over a single weekend. As the name says: It enables to manage networks and the connected devices from any authorized PC. It also allows the controlling of the failing encryption 'monsters'.
The salesman of the encryption machines first asks reproachfully: "Is he allowed to do this?" The technically not very informed gentleman received a horror answer from all network-oriented co-workers.

Soon, every wireless telephone will need a chip to encrypt the spoken words. Because the conversation runs through the air and can be heard by everybody.

Encryption? There are always a lot of secrets involves with it. Later, the company which made and delivered its 'monsters' was deeply involved in rumors, mystery intrigues, and other wild stories. And had, to say it mildly, a very inglorious end.

Quote: "Money does not stink. Petunia non-olet".

11.7. The ATM and other Flops.

Grandpa, stop the idiotic trying to predict the future! Go back to the more or less bearable everyday life!
Here, again once more, new technologies are waiting impatiently for him. Of course, the Institution must use it immediately. They want to avoid being behind the moon, where they were at the time he had joined them.

162

What now came was for him most likely the last new data transmission protocol he had to learn: The ATM (Asynchronous Transmission Mode). This is an asynchronous broadband method for data communications. That means the simultaneous transmission of data, voice, pictures, and video is possible. As with the ISDN, but with far higher throughput capacity. It is by far the most complicated of all the Data Communication protocols he encountered until now.

He was sent to attend an intensive one-week training seminar in Vienna. For the course, he needed the approval of his bosses. The high cost of the training had to be approved by a three-level, higher-up chief. Unnecessary expenses should be avoided if possible. To adhere to the institute's rules of conduct. The big boss was very critical concerning training costs. He immediately asks the following question: "What does our man have to do with ATM? These are banknote distributing machines and which those we have nothing to do with". He meant the 'Automatic Teller Machine'. The abbreviation for them is also ATM. His group leader had to 'educate' the boss. ATM as a transmission media was only known to insiders and not to bosses. And very often, not just this time, technical abbreviations are not unique.

Configuring an ATM net is a nightmare for any telecommunication specialist. This protocol is by far the most complicated that he has ever come across. It uses an addressing method with addresses with the length of twenty or even more digits. The instructor in Vienna said: "It is a pure miracle that something like this works at all".
It is a connection-oriented protocol. The opposite is the connection-less technologies such as Ethernet and TCP/IP. Or the USB (Universal Serial Bus) as it is used today in every PC and others to connect very nearby components such as a keyboard, mouse, printer, etc. to the CPU. Every connected device can send and receive at any time. When the bus is overloaded, then the device is forced to try it over and over again.

The only positive thing in the week in Vienna was his visit to the Prater. It was not enough time to drink a glass of wine in a 'Heurigen' in Grinzing. He really would have needed one or more good swigs. He was absolutely 'done' after the course.

ATM did not make a real breakthrough in computer-to-computer data communication. Because it is by far too complex. Why? Again designed by a committee: By the CCITT (Comité Consultatif International Téléphonique et Télégraphique) and then later the ITU-T (International Telecommunication Union).

In his humble opinion: ATM was a complete flop.

Like many other technical 'wonders':
.
The Tower of Babel.
The Vasa. A Swedish military ship in the 17th century.
The Zeppelin.
The Ford Edsel.
The Eidophor.
The Wankel engine.
The vertical starting fighter airplanes.
Concorde.
etc.

A non-technical flop will now follow. And this story will explain why the servers at the Institution had glacier names.
The server computers installed there used the UNIX operating system. Now, these servers must be given a name. As anonymous as possible because an outsider should not find out where the device is located or for what it is used. The for the server's responsible manager asked his colleagues to suggest an appropriate naming concept.
He was asked too. That day he was 'pissed' off. Why? This doesn't matter. In the staff restaurant, he was now asked for an idea. Intuitively and because of being in a terribly bad, cold mood, he said tersely: "Give them glaciers names".
Which they did. Until today, he is still ashamed of his idea and hoped since then that no one would ever find out that he built

this 'shit'. Because it is extremely uncomfortable to address the servers with long names such as the Aletschgletscher, Rhonegletscher, and such IGauligletescher. And so on.

(PS: Is his book in German with the title: 'Mit dem Computer per DU' not also a flop?)

11.8. The OSI-ISO Model.

A more pleasant topic is what will be described now. It was, not so early, realized that the many different data communication protocols will lead to an uncontrolled situation. The routers were able to handle this. Mostly.
This 'salad' of data communication protocols awakened memories of what he had to eat when he was a child. So, 75 years ago. It was called 'Birchermüesli'. Invented by a certain Dr. Bircher in Zurich. This is mainly breakfast food, mainly for children vegetarians, and vegans freaks. Made of cereals, milk, and fruits. Mixing all this together results in 'oatmeal'. Such as the situation in the data communication world was at the time before the OSI-ISO model.

A structure to make the interconnection between protocols clearer and easier was badly needed. As a big exception, an international organization manages, with the cooperation of the private industry, to achieve this: The OSI-ISO model.

This is not a play of letters. It stands for Open System Interconnection (OSI) and the International Standard Organization (ISO).
It is also known as the seven-layer model. Is it comparable to: 'The Seven Pillars of Wisdom'? (A book written by Lawrence of Arabia). Or even to the seven wonders of the Antique world?

Nonsense. Again, one of his unconscious associations.

The seven layers;

Layer 1: Bit Transmission (Physical Layer).
Layer 2: Delivery on the last branch of a connection (Link Layer).
Layer 3: Network (Network Layer).
Layer 4: Transport (Transport Layer).
Layer 5: Session (Session Layer).
Layer 6: Presentation (Presentation Layer).
Layer 7: Application (Application Layer).

Details description of the layers:

Drawer 1: This layer provides mechanical, electrical, and other functions to activate or deactivate physical connections, maintain them, and transmit bits. These may be, for example, electrical signals, optical signals (lasers rays), radio waves (wireless networks), or sounds
.
Drawer 2: The task is to provide a reliable, substantially error-free transmission of the data packet. It has to guarantee and regulate access to the transmission medium by packing the bit data stream into blocks. Then also adding check-sums to the packets. Defective blocks can be recognized by the receiver and either discarded or even corrected.

Drawer 3: It ensures the switching of connections for line-oriented services and the forwarding of data packets for packet-oriented services. In both cases, the data transmission goes over the entire communication network and includes the search for the route (routing) between the network nodes. There is not always direct communication possible between sender and destination. The packets are forwarded by those nodes.

Drawer 4: The tasks of the transport layer include segmenting the data stream and congestion avoidance, and to guide the data packet through the net.

Drawer 5: This ensures process communication between two

systems. Among other things, the protocol RPC (remote procedure call) can be found here. To resolve session breakdowns and similar problems, the session layer provides organized and synchronized services. For this purpose, so-called fixed points (checkpoints) are introduced, at which the session can be synchronized again after a transport connection has failed, without the transmission having to start again.

Drawer 6: This converts the system-dependent representation of the data (e.g. ASCII, EBCDIC) into an independent form and thus enables the syntactically correct data exchange between different systems. Tasks such as data compression and encryption also belong to layer 6.

Drawer 7: Services, applications, and network management. The application layer provides functions for applications. This layer creates the connection to the lower layers. Data entry and output also take place at this level. The applications themselves do not belong to the layer.

Quote: "Knowledge is power. To know nothing does also not matters".

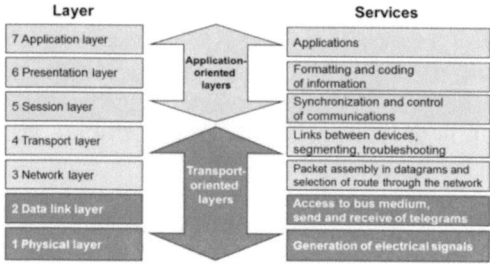

80. The OSI-ISO Model

11.9. A 'parable' of the OSI-ISO model.

Trying to explain the layer model to non-computer-oriented normal folks is rather cumbersome. A plausible comparison of the OSI-ISO structure with them in real life possible facts is the following:

Layer 7: A man is sitting in a bar in the city. The restaurant is known as a place to start a flirt. It is exactly his actual motivation to be there. (Application layer).

Layer 6: A beautiful lady is sitting in the other corner of the bar: She is presenting very well. With subtle makeup, in a white blouse, black silken skirt, and classic high heels. (Presentation layer).

Layer 5: The man starts a conversation. As usual, the first theme is the current weather. Soon, also very common, they chat about the astrological signs of the zodiac. The man offers her a glass of French champagne. Not 'just' an Italian 'Prosecco'. (Session layer).

Layer 4: The man suggested the lady to go to a more elegant restaurant with decent music. She agrees. "Which means of

168

transport shall we use? Own car, taxi or public conveyances?" (Transport layer).

Layer 3: They take the public transport media. "What is the fastest and least congested route?" (Network layer).

Layer 2: The conversation continues lively, and not only that. In German, one would say: The 'chemistry' between the two is perfect. Even without pharmaceuticals. It's getting late. The restaurant closes. They take a taxi to the house where she lives. At the entrance, she asks: "Are you coming up for a coffee or a glass of wine?" Stupid question: "Very, very much so". Then they go to her apartment (Link layer).

Layer 1: (Physical layer).

Have you got that? Haben Sie es verstanden?_Vous l'avez? Ce l'hai fatta?_¿Entendiste eso? Har du förtaat?

Epilogue.

After lots of parables, phrases, theses, illusions, and quotes everything was said. Or better: Written. That's it!

Maybe...

After 2004 the live 'Other Computer History' stops for him. Even if the internet euphoria and computer mania only then started their furious success on the planet earth. Today, it's the daily bread for almost everybody. And it often also results in daily anger. Computers are portable in every woman's purse and in each man's trousers bag. All-time ready. As was said and still is the slogan of the Boy Scouts.

Or even not so ready. Because the accumulator is 'weak' (low)! That it does not come so far there is in the public trains and soon also in every public restroom a socket to charge it. For free! What was in 1964 required space in size of a gymnastic hall for data storage and costsi millions, are today to have on a chip of 50x10x5 millimeter in size. For about ten dollars. The clock rate of the computer is in the gigahertz range. In computer communication, we are today from the 50 baud rate in 1955 to the terabits. This is a number with a one at the beginning, followed by eleven zeros.
From the point-to-point connections to the global worldwide network. Everyone is everywhere on the globe, always online. Does everyone want this?

He, for example, NOT

And what is going on over the internet? Mostly, spam, garbage, unwanted advertisements, harassment, and pornography are floating' around. Thanks to the anonymity of the sender.
Grandpa, you should keep silent! There are not only negatives to say about the internet. There are also a lot of reasonable benefits possible to get by the net. Whatever one understands by 'reasonable'. This is like everything on earth: Relative. Positive is for example E-mail to nearby or distant friends.

Searching for forgotten facts, unknown terms, and so on. Thanks to Google and Wikipedia! Ordering toner for an outdated laser printer. Save him the tedious phoning around to find one. Also filling in questionnaires from reasonable surveys. Listen to the radio, watch TV, chat over voicemail, and so on. To try to find over the net more or less useful information.

A long-overdue quote: "The computer never becomes human. Humanity gets more and more 'computerotic'". (H.Aemmerli)

Please, Grandpa, enough of your critics! You better keep your 'pseudo-philosophic associations' for yourself.

Could you have written this book without a word processor? Even if the text processing programs often had problems with his text. Especially with his often very special Swiss German expressions. The language translation programs were unable to translate words like 'Zurichdeutsch', 'Zwanziger 'and phrases like: 'Ich verstehe nur Bahnhof' the way he wanted.

The computer as a job killer? Of course not. Because they must be developed, manufactured, sold, packet, and delivered. Let alone the millions of man-years to create the programs and applications. He cannot stop applying quotes. For example: "The past doesn't let us go, the future worries us, and therefore we cannot enjoy the present". (Unknown author)

Followed by his Quote: "The future could for example be the premature doomsday caused by a 'bug' in an artificial Intelligent (AT) program for military applications".

For him, most of today's computer applications have in reality a frightening short 'halftime' value.
But it is reassuring to know that even the latest computer with a fraction of a nanosecond technology still works with the same simple principle of 'and' 'or' 'nand' 'nor', 'xor' and 'xnor' logic. Only the number of individual switching elements in a processor has risen from thousands to billions.

But the technology is today at its borders. The conductor tracks in the microchips have been reduced to the size of a few atoms. Where is the limit of bandwidth in telecommunication? Surely somewhere... And surely there, is also for it one day a limit.

Whatever will come is not really important to him. And therefore he doesn't worry.
Humanity still believes that one day everything will be explainable. The universe with billions of galaxies, stars, planets, comets, and meteorites. The human brain, with 80 billion brain cells and millions of kilometers of nerve fibers. (Scientifically explained in 2019).

Absolute arrogance...

Have you got that? Haben Sie es verstanden? Vous l'avez? Ce l'hai fatta? ¿Entendiste eso? Har du förtaat?

The last quote: "The more that he knows, the more he knows that he knows nothing".

How I became a Programmer (by Stephan Bodmer).

When I was a child, my mother used some peculiar paper to write her grocery shopping list. It was a small sheet of hard paper with a small list of numbers and holes on it (was it a list of 16 or 32 numbers per line, I don't remember). When I asked her what the numbers meant, she told me that my father gave her these paper sheets, and it was something from work and has to do with computers.

A few years later, my father brought me on a Saturday morning to his workplace at CERN in Geneva. He had to do some work there. I accompanied him. I arrived at a huge room with large closets. They were filled with electronic components. Then there were machines with fast-rolling magnetic tapes. There were a dozen of these machines. The room was cool and noisy. A strong air conditioning system was active. We went to the control room, and he put me in front of a computer screen and loaded a pinball game to keep me quiet. I played a bit. But I was more interested in all the computers around me. I found a strange 'typewriter' machine in a corner with some paper sheets on it.
Then, it hit me! It was the same paper that my mother used to write her grocery list on it. I looked more into it and it was fascinating. I believe to think to myself that it was at that moment (was I six or eight years old ?) that I decided to become a 'programmer/analyst' like my father.

A few years later, my father bought me my first computer. It was a Commodore Vic-20. I passed many months learning and writing my programs on this machine. The first game that I called 'submarine' was never finished because I hit the available memory limit quite fast (the machine had only 3.5 KB of memory for BASIC programs). My father bought me the Commodore 64 a few years later. This one was a blast. Everybody who grows up with this machine knows what I am talking about. I could write my programs without memory constraints. I could also play games. Tons of games and it was so much fun. I still remember playing 'Ultima IV' (by Richard

Gariott) for over a year. As I did not understand English at that time. I had to write down all the 'dialogs' of the game. My father could translate it for me later in the afternoon. This game opened my mind and imagination like no other game before. It was a revelation to me. I did never thank my father enough for bringing me this game back from the United States when he was on a professional trip. I also wrote my first 'demo' and I was so proud of it. At my school, we were a bunch of friends with the same 'computer enthusiasm' attitude. I showed one of my demos to a friend, then he told me it was quite slow but if you code it in machine language it will run faster.

I was intrigued. What was he talking about?

He showed me a 'compiler' he wrote to translate the BASIC program to machine language. I was completely astounded. My demo runs a lot faster after converting it to machine language with his compiler. The same night, I asked my father to explain to me what machine language was.

A few years later it started to become serious. My father bought me an Amiga 2000 so that I could work on it for my studies. I learned to program in Modula-2, C, and C++ on this amazing computer. At Geneva University, in my computer history class, I learned all that I needed to understand computer science. A peculiar machine intrigued me. It was the 'Hollerith machine'. This machine was the one I found many years ago in the control room of my father's workplace, which looked like a typewriter. Then it hit me again. My father was part of the computer revolution!

A few years later I became a 'programmer' just like my father and he and I started to talk about our experiences as computer engineers and all the problems we had to face daily. Then he started to tell me his stories and experiences from his past. It was so amazing to hear him talk about it. As a computer person myself I was hooked on his lips, I could understand what he was talking about and it was so inspiring to hear from a 'first hand' what the 'computer revolution was in the 'field'. I understood quite rapidly that his knowledge of past computer history could interest many people. So, I suggested

174

to him to write a book about it so that everyone (not only me) could enjoy his stories.
I would like to thank my father for sharing these amazing computer stories with us.
Thanks, Dad, for making my childhood with computers such a wonderful time.

Pictures Index

PS:

Urgent recommendation:

To be present in every computer room, Office, and everywhere when a computer is involved:

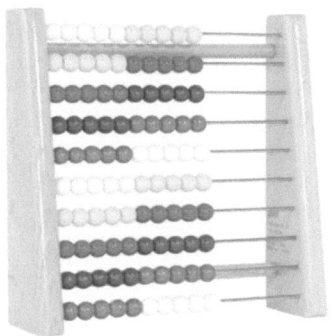

81. The First Aid Kit